Skinny or Not,
Here I Come

Skinny or Not, Here I Come

A Memoir of an Eating Disorder
and Recovery Journey

Margaret Cupit-Link

RESOURCE *Publications* • Eugene, Oregon

SKINNY OR NOT, HERE I COME
A Memoir of an Eating Disorder and Recovery Journey

Copyright © 2020 MargaretCupit-Link. All rights reserved. Except for brief quotations in critical publications or reviews, no part of this book may be reproduced in any manner without prior written permission from the publisher. Write: Permissions, Wipf and Stock Publishers, 199 W. 8th Ave., Suite 3, Eugene, OR 97401.

Resource Publications
An Imprint of Wipf and Stock Publishers
199 W. 8th Ave., Suite 3
Eugene, OR 97401

www.wipfandstock.com

PAPERBACK ISBN: 978-1-7252-8393-0
HARDCOVER ISBN: 978-1-7252-8392-3
EBOOK ISBN: 978-1-7252-8394-7

Manufactured in the U.S.A.   10/30/20

Scripture quotations taken from the New American Standard Bible ® (NASB), Copyright © 1960, 1962, 1963, 1968, 1971, 1972, 1973, 1975, 1977, 1995 by The Lockman Foundation. Used by permission. www.Lockman.org.

Rohr, Richard. *Breathing under Water: Spirituality and the Twelve Steps.* London: Society for Promoting Christian Knowledge, 2018. "Copyright © 2018 by CAC. Used by permission of CAC. All rights reserved worldwide."

Contents

Introduction | vii

1. The Beginning | 1
2. After Anorexia | 14
3. College, Cancer, and Control | 21
4. Low Points at Low Weights | 31
5. Recovery | 42
6. Relapses | 52
7. Eating Disorders, God, and Addiction | 64
8. Lessons Learned | 74

Bibliography | 83

Introduction

My decision to share the details of my eating disorder through writing has been years in the making. For a long time, I only wanted to share with readers if I could come from a place of wisdom and success, as a fully-recovered individual. Once I truly began to recover, though, I realized that "fully-recovered" was not what my readers deserved; it was honesty.

Admittedly, some of my hesitation came from a place of pride. How much of this would be "too much" for people to handle? Would I embarrass myself? Would I embarrass my family? Some of my hesitation came from a fear of commitment to the cause. I wasn't ready to give up my eating disorder completely because there were times that I liked what it did for me. If I published this, I would have to stop lying to myself and the world. I would have to stop pretending everything was perfect when things were really hard, stop scrutinizing every picture of myself of social media to be sure I looked "skinny enough", and stop dieting as a coping mechanism for my feelings. I hadn't yet come to the full realization that my eating disorder was an addiction, or if I had, I wasn't quite ready to get rid of it.

As I began to write, I began to understand. As I began to understand, I began to heal. As I began to heal, I began to believe that my struggle was not unique. My struggle is like that of countless others who suffer from debilitating self hatred and unhealthy eating patterns that keep them from reaching their full potential in

Introduction

life. Because of this, I could not allow my recovery to be private, to be merely about me. It had to be shared.

Most of the names in this text have been changed. Exceptions include my life-changing eating disorder therapist (Gina), heroic dietitian (Maiya), and sisters (Sissy and Flynn), who have given me permission to use their first names.

Anorexia

She yells, She screams,
Criticizing all she sees.
Her hopes, Her dreams
Looking into the mirror
Crying hysterically.
Nothing is perfect,
Therefore it is no good.
Hating her reflection,
Everything she sees.
Unsatisfied from within
Searching for fulfillment
Crying out with rage.
As I sit and listen,
Helpless and amazed.
So much potential,
A great life unlived.
All she can't see
Is what truly is:
Beauty and grace.
She sees disgrace,
Not kindness and care;
She's in despair.
Talented and smart,
She lives in the dark,
Breaking my heart.

— 1 —

The Beginning

I CANNOT PINPOINT THE exact moment in time when I became conscious of my body as a separate entity from myself, as something I needed to control. I do, however, remember the year that these thoughts first took over my life.

I was in sixth grade, twelve years old. It was the age that little girls started noticing each other's outfits, having crushes on boys, wearing a hint of mascara on special occasions, and being catty. Everyone was wearing *Abercrombie and Fitch* to school, and it suddenly seemed important for clothes to broadcast their brand names. I got braces in the early fall, and I had to get glasses shortly thereafter. On top of that, I didn't own any *Abercrombie*. For most of my life, I'd been surrounded by tons of friends without ever making an effort, but things had changed. I was acutely aware that I was neither popular nor beautiful, and both of these things bothered me.

My mom had gone back to teaching school at the beginning of that school year. She had been a stay-at-home mom for as long as I could remember, but she'd started working again when my little sister was old enough to go to school, and I was selfishly (and secretly) very disappointed. Mama had less time for me. I felt like she was being taken away from me. She was no longer home whenever I was home, and she had much less time to cook and clean, pack lunches, and do our laundry. She could no longer come to every field trip and tennis practice, and she often seemed stressed at the end of the school day. To make matters worse, instead of doing parent pick-up, I had to ride the school bus between the elementary school where she taught and my middle school, which was embarrassing.

It was the year that girls started gossiping. On the days that it rained, recess was moved into the gym. On one of these days, I sat next to the girl with no friends and talked to her because she seemed sad, and the other girls gave me weird looks. On another day, I walked up to a group of girls standing in a circle, and all of them quickly became silent. I knew they were talking about me, and I could sense that they didn't want me to join them. All of that was hard, but none of it was about my body, at least not at first.

It was also the year that my thighs began to thicken and I needed a training bra for my new tiny breast buds that had seemingly popped up overnight. There were four of us in my tennis group, and I remember my mom saying that all of us were starting to "fill out," except for my friend Angela. She was long and lanky and had no curves. I don't know if I thought that "filling out" was a bad thing, if I thought Angela's body was more beautiful because it was not curvy, or if I was simply afraid of change. I viewed the process of bodily development as sad, unfortunate, and unattractive. I started to compare my body to all of my friends' bodies. In the back of the car on the way to a tennis tournament, I sat with my friend, Angela, in our tennis skirts, I noticed our adjacent thighs pressed firmly against the leather seats. Mine were bigger. It was something I hadn't noticed before, but once I did, I noticed it every time I sat down. I wondered if that was why boys liked her more.

Another fall day, I sat in the backseat of an SUV with my good friend, Marilyn. She had transferred to a private school, so I didn't see her at school any more. She had always been what my mother called "a beanpole," because she was very thin without a trace of curves. As Marilyn and I waited for her mom to finish running errands, we stayed in the car and ate girl scout cookies. After each of us had a few of the chocolate peanut butter cookies, Marilyn closed the box and said, "No offense, but you don't

The Beginning

need any more of these." When I reflect on it today, I am sure that it was Marilyn's mother's voice that was coming out, not hers. It was something her weight-conscious mother had said a thousand times about cookies. In that moment, as a vulnerable and insecure twelve-year-old sitting next to a skinny friend, it hurt. This pain solidified the very vague and intermittent idea I'd had about my body; it wasn't good enough. I had found an explanation for why I sometimes felt insecure around my classmates.

Marilyn was not the only person to influence my body image, nor was she the first. Her words were echoes of our superficial southern culture, a culture that had also impacted our mothers. While I can't speak for all mothers, I know that my mother did not want to teach me to dislike myself or my body in any way. Mama wanted me to be happy and healthy above all else, and she strove to teach me to be kind to myself whenever I was a supreme perfectionist. Still, I know that I'm not alone when I say that I learned that being thin was an important value from my mother. Throughout most of my childhood, Mama did not eat meals with us. She cooked family dinners but then sipped on unsweetened iced tea while we ate. She never ordered herself anything except for Diet Coke when we went to fast food restaurants. She often ate meal replacement bars or shakes for breakfast or lunch. Every once in a while, she would buy a birthday cake and eat most of it the following night. I never thought much about it. I just thought it was how grown-up women ate.

A few weeks after getting braces on my teeth, I tried on some new blue jeans that my mom had picked out for me. I walked around the living room, modeling the jeans, liking the way they felt. "You look like you've slimmed down lately," she said. Not only was I thrilled to have her attention on me at the end of a busy school day, but I also felt like I was making her proud. Up until that point, I had not lost weight on purpose. I had been eating lots of soft foods because my teeth hurt from the new braces. It felt like a very important compliment, though, and it made me feel confident and powerful. If weight loss had been so easy for me in just a few short weeks, I was sure I could be even better at it if I tried.

Skinny or Not, Here I Come

Just a couple of months later, it was Lent. My sisters and I went to weekly classes on Wednesday nights at the small Catholic church in town. It was held in an old school building across the street from the church which had not been renovated since the 1970s. We went to class for an hour with other kids in the same grade then visited with the rest of the kids at a Lenten dinner provided by the church. I took my classes seriously. It was an extension of my perfectionism and my academic performance. At that point in my life, I hadn't developed my spirituality very much, but I was very morally scrupulous. I wanted to be good at everything I did, and my faith was no exception.

During the Lenten season, we took a break from reciting memorized Catholic prayers and learned about fasting. Giving up food sounded horrible, which made it even more of a "sacrifice" for God. The more I thought about the importance of fasting in Lent, the more I wanted to be good at it. I also knew it would benefit my appearance. I can still clearly remember the crucifix hanging in the sanctuary of the church, large and wooden. Jesus wore nothing but a loin cloth, and his hands and feet were pierced with nails, dripping with bright red blood. His hair was long and brown, framing his face. He gazed downwards with a sad expression. What I remember most, though, was his rib cage. I could count every bone. It reminded me of the verse in the book of Psalms that is thought to refer to Jesus: "I can count all my bones. They look, they stare at me: They divide my garments among them, And for my clothing they cast lots."[1] The more I looked at the crucifix, the more I saw Christ's protruding bones as evidence of his obedience to God.

Our Girl Scout troop meetings were sometimes held at the church as well. Soon after Lent began, I found myself making different judgments about certain foods as bad or less bad. I had not really judged food in that way before I started fasting. Food was just food, and all of it served the same basic purpose. At one of the meetings, I surveyed the options: potato chips or Girl Scout cookies (there was always a surplus of these because our mothers bought the majority of the cookies we sold). I loved sweets more

---

1. Psalm 22:17–18

The Beginning

than anything, so I chose chips. That single serving bag of corn chips was a stepping stone for me. From that point on, I thought before I ate. Although I was thoughtful, I wasn't practicing mindfulness; I was scrutinizing every bite and calorie I consumed.

Soon, other people started to comment on my weight. I heard adults tell my mom that I was "getting a nice figure" and my classmates refer to me as "skinny." Getting positive attention for my physical appearance was foreign to me, but I loved it. I was used to being the smart one who got called onto stage for medals at the school award ceremony, the goofy one with a "great personality" who got the funny roles in the school play, the kind one who tried to be inclusive of the outcasts. It was nice to finally feel like the pretty one, and I felt like I'd achieved my Lenten goal. I was happy with myself, and I wanted to make sure I didn't gain the weight back. Over the next several months, I ate slowly and cautiously, as I had when my braces were new, with the goal of maintaining my new weight.

In addition to dieting, there were other changes I made that Lent that I viewed as "Christ-like" at the time but now view as self abusive. In an effort to "help" my mom with her job, and in retrospect, spend more time with her, I gave myself tasks to do in her classroom. Before school, I manually sharpened pencils until my hands blistered. After school, I strained myself placing chairs on desktops in preparation for the janitor to sweep the room. At home, I packed lunches for my mom and my sisters. I chopped apples and pears, made sandwiches, and filled plastic bags with chips. Although everyone was thankful for the lunches, no one knew my alternative motive: spending time with the food. As I deprived myself of food, I yearned for it. If I wasn't eating it, at least I could smell it, touch it, and see it.

For myself, I always packed a less-tempting lunch: a meal replacement bar that my mom kept in the pantry and a handful of green grapes. I ate everything slowly and carefully, taking the tiniest of bites; it lasted longer this way and made me feel full faster. The moment my stomach felt remotely satisfied, I ended my meal by throwing it in the trash. "I'm so full," I would say to the people at my lunch table. My hunger was most severe during the last period of the day, algebra. Luckily, I was great at math and didn't need to pay very much attention in order to get good grades in the class. As I felt my stomach growl, I reminded myself that I would be able to eat again at dinner time. After school, I filled up on diet soda, which temporarily stopped the pain. It took me a long time to notice the gradual changes that were happening to my body: the physical weakness, mental fogginess, and sensitivity to cold. Perhaps the first time I recognized these sensations was on a trip with my friend Heidi.

It was on a trip to Heidi's dance competition that I discovered what a hunger pain was. We stayed in a hotel, and because I had only picked at my meals, I was very hungry at bedtime. The first phase of hunger is a growling stomach feeling, but there comes a period where that fades away and you forget you're hungry, and the next phase is actually painful. I would lie awake for several hours after everyone had gone to bed. It's almost impossible to fall asleep when you're hungry (this is why infants don't sleep through the night; they need to eat to feel comfortable). At the time, I convinced myself that this was what skinny people did; they didn't snack between meals, and they ignored their hunger. I thought that it would get better if I got used to it. Surely my friends Marilyn and Angela had felt this way before, I told myself.

The next day, we visited the indoor pool, which was supposedly heated. All of the girls at the dance competition were swimming. I looked around at all of them, sizing them up, assessing the size of their thighs or the flatness of their bellies or the extent to which their hip bones jutted out. I had to be the skinniest in order to be as pretty as they were, I told myself. I didn't have the privilege of not having the most beautiful body because my face was less beautiful. I looked down at my body, and seeing my ribs, I felt pride. The pool was miserably cold. Chill bumps sprouted up all over my skin, and no matter how much I swam around, I couldn't get warm. Luckily, there was a steam room. I sat in it for the entire time, unable to play with my friends because I was too cold to swim. I didn't understand why the others didn't seem to be cold.

The Beginning

The breakfast buffet at the hotel was glorious. I realized that buffets were ideal because I could fill my plate with beautiful foods as if none of them were off limits and savor them with my eyes and my sense of smell. I carefully selected pancakes with syrup, a pastry, eggs, fruit salad, and hash browns. I cut everything into tiny pieces and took tiny tastes of each item. I noticed that Heidi's mom was watching, so I pushed everything around my plate and went back for seconds. I wanted it to look like I was eating. It would be embarrassing to admit that I was on a diet. After that trip, Heidi's mom told my mom that I wasn't eating enough. Mama asked me if I was trying to lose weight, and I said no. I wasn't lying; I didn't even know how much I weighed, and I didn't have a plan to lose more weight. I just knew that I felt so powerful after losing that little bit of weight, and I was not going to risk gaining any of it back.

It became apparent to my family that there was a serious problem when the school nurse sent me home from school early one day. I was in algebra when I felt a sinking sensation and saw the room getting dark. When I stood up, I almost passed out. In the nurse's office, my blood pressure was low, and so was my heart rate. She told me I'd had a vasovagal episode. I was instructed to drink a cup of water and lie down as I waited for my ride. When I reached Mama's classroom, she briskly walked to the door to greet me. She told me that I looked pale. Holding my hands in hers, she noted that they were freezing and my fingernails were a shade of purple. She took me down the hall to see her school nurse, Rose.

My mom quickly explained to her that I had almost fainted at school and pointed out my fingernails to her. "Do her nails look purple to you?"

After taking one glance at me, Nurse Rose replied, "She looks very thin. Have you weighed her lately?" My mom shook her head no. The nurse guided us into her office and had me step on the scale. I weighed seventy pounds. This didn't mean anything to me. I had never owned a scale, and growing up I'd only weighed myself at the doctor's office. I saw the nurse and my mother exchange concerned glances.

"I thought she was just getting thinner because she had a growth spurt," Mama explained.

"This is probably why her heart rate is low," Nurse Rose said, sadness in her voice. Years later, I learned that one of her daughters had struggled with anorexia.

When we left, I could tell my mom was worried about me. She took me to the local pediatrician. We explained the near-fainting-episode story to him. He told us it sounded like orthostatic hypotension, or episodic low blood pressure when going from sitting to standing. My mom asked, "Could weight loss cause low blood pressure?"

"Possibly, if it was a lot," the doctor said.

"Can someone be anorexic at this age?" Mama was thinking about it more than he was.

"It would be very unlikely. She is only twelve," he responded. My mom looked relieved for a moment. The doctor then asked my mom to leave the room so he could ask me a few questions in private.

"Have you been trying to lose weight?" he asked me.

"No," I said, not elaborating. I wasn't lying. I had not been trying to lose weight. I had just been desperately trying to prevent weight gain.

"Do you want to be thinner?" he continued.

"No." Again, this was not a lie. I didn't need to be any thinner. I just didn't want to be fatter, either.

"Have you had pain in your belly?"

"Sometimes it hurts to eat," I admitted. I didn't explain that I just got full really fast, so anything more than a few bites was uncomfortable.

"How are you sleeping?" he went on.

"Fine," I pretended. I often woke up in the middle of the night with a growling stomach, but that was part of my Lenten promise. I envisioned Christ on the cross, with every rib visible.

The doctor told my mom that I did not have an eating disorder. I was too young, and I clearly wasn't trying to lose weight, so

The Beginning

it was probably due to another health issue. He had the nurse draw some of my blood for labs and referred me to the hospital for a test.

A few days later, my grandmother took me to the hospital so my mom didn't have to miss school. She sat with me in the waiting room. Once I was called into the back, I had to swallow a white, pasty substance prior to having some x-rays taken. I now know this as an upper gastrointestinal series. We were quickly notified that the study results were normal. I was not surprised, but I was a little disappointed, because it would have been easier to be skinny if I had a medical problem. My grandmother, who is a counseling psychologist, did not look relieved. I wonder if the test confirmed her suspicions.

"Are you starving yourself?" my grandmother asked. She was the first person to ever ask me this question.

"I don't know," I answered honestly, because I had never thought of it that way. That phrase sounded malicious and scary. I did not think I was harming myself. I was just excelling at something that all of society honored as good and impressive but few people could pull off. I was still eating *something* at every meal. I was still thinking about food and smelling food and looking at food. So much of my day was about food. How could that be starving myself?

After all of the blood work came back as normal, my grandmother and my mother were convinced that I had anorexia. It was helpful to have my grandmother's expertise. I sometimes wonder how long it would have taken for me to be diagnosed if my family didn't know so much about mental illness. They began observing me at supper time. It was a relief at first. I would cut my food up in tiny pieces and push it around my plate, as I had become accustomed to doing. Then, after taking a few small and bites and becoming full, I would stop eating, even though I wanted more. One of them would say something like, "two more bites of green beans and two more bites of chicken." With that, I would give myself permission to take the number of bites I was instructed to take, but no more. I wanted those extra bites, but I also liked how it felt to be doted on.

Next, they asked my teachers about my eating at school and expressed their concern. My sixth grade science teacher said, "I've always thought she did a good job at lunch."

I suppose this was in reference to the grapes and meal replacement bars. Did she know that I'd been eating less and less of them each day? Did she know that I often took home half of a bar and brought the same one back in my lunchbox the next day? Did she know that when I ran out of bars I ate only grapes? Did she know that I could bite a grape into at least four pieces so that one grape lasted as long as four grapes normally would? Clearly she did not know these things.

I was eventually told by both my mom and grandmother that I had two options. I could either eat what I was instructed to eat and go to see a psychologist who specialized in eating disorders once a week, or I could go to an inpatient treatment center for girls with eating disorders. I took the first option because I did not think I needed to go to a hospital; I didn't even think I had a problem. I believed that I had found a way to feel good about myself and needed to learn to maintain my weight instead of losing more so that others didn't worry about me, so I did what my family required of me while holding onto my eating disorder as much as I could.

Barbara was a psychologist an hour away from my hometown. Her office was calming with meditative music in the waiting room. She was also very skinny, which made me feel reassured that she would be alright with me being skinny. She began the appointment by getting a blind weight, having me stand on the scale facing backwards so that I couldn't see the number.

We then sat in her office, me on a couch, and her in a chair, while she sipped a Diet Coke. I don't remember much of what we talked about. She showed me some diagrams that illustrated body dysmorphia. She asked me to point to which silhouette most resembled my body habitus. I picked one. She told me that I was wrong and said I resembled a thinner one. I was disappointed that she didn't point to the very thinnest one, which looked like a concentration camp victim. She asked me which body type I

The Beginning

thought men were most attracted to. I pointed to one. She pointed to a much bigger one. This didn't persuade me. I didn't want to be skinny because of what men liked. I wanted to be skinny because *I* liked it.

My family monitored all of my meals, including those at school. This was the humiliating part. At lunch time, I had to sit with the school nurse away from the rest of the class. She was way worse than my mother or grandmother. Instead of compromising with me by telling me to eat a few more bites, she told me to eat most of what was on my plate. It felt like a huge amount of food. Although I was disgusted by the amount of school cafeteria food I was expected to eat, I could do it. I wasn't the one responsible if I gained weight, I reminded myself; that was someone else's fault. I know now that I faked my way through recovery. I ate only the bites I was told to eat, and when I was in charge of planning my own meals, I only chose "healthy" foods. This was another way for me to be good at something, to succeed. There were good foods and bad foods, and I wasn't going to eat the bad foods.

Being embarrassed at school was not the only way I was punished for having an eating disorder. I wasn't allowed to continue playing tennis until I gained a certain amount of weight. Because I didn't want to do anything but eat the bare minimum, I just quit tennis. I have always wondered how different things would have been for me if I had eaten more, gained weight, and kept playing tennis. Perhaps I would have been a great tennis player. There was also a visit with my pediatrician after my therapy had started, during a time in which I was only eating what I was required to eat and not a bite more. He recorded my weight weekly, and I was down a couple of pounds from the week before. My mom mentioned that cheerleading tryouts were going on, and he recommended that I not participate. I must have begged my mom to give me another chance, because I kept going to tryouts. I did not make the cheerleading team that year. I wasn't even that upset about it. "At least I'm skinnier than all the girls who made the team," I told myself.

I slowly began to gain weight, feel physically stronger, and come up with my own meal plans. However, I never discussed or considered the reasons I had developed an eating disorder. Barbara taught me how to recognize the "eating disorder voice" and then imagine myself fighting against it, slashing it with a sword, silencing it. I learned to silence the thoughts and follow my meal plan. However, I was never asked why I wanted to be thin or, more importantly, what mattered more to me than being thin. When I reached the point in my recovery where no one had to force me to eat, Barbara invited me to attend an eating disorder support group. It was mostly girls a little older than me, high school age. Barbara told me that some of them had anorexia, and others had bulimia. I remember her telling me that some of the girls were underweight, some a healthy weight, and some even overweight. The support group was kind and welcoming to me. We sat in a circle on the floor in a large room. I looked around, amazed at how different our bodies could be. I scanned the room, judging each girl based on her weight, feeling proud that I was the thinnest one. I was surprised to learn that there were people out there who shared a desire to control their weight but were not underweight. I never imagined that I would one day become one of them.

One of the biggest challenges to my early recovery came soon after. My older sister developed an eating disorder after she started high school. I started questioning her weight loss before everyone else did. For as long as I could remember, she had never been super thin. She had always been athletic, friendly, and popular; she didn't *need* to be skinny to be those things. After she lost the first ten pounds, people complimented her left and right. It was as if all of a sudden everyone realized how beautiful she was. I watched her closely, analyzing her food choices, noticing that she went to the gym to run every single day. I told my mom and grandmother that I was worried, but they dismissed it. I think they were happy to see that she'd become thin. Mama said, "She eats a large grilled chicken salad every day, and even if that's the only thing she eats, that's enough calories to survive."

When I told my sister that I was concerned about her, she asked me not to worry. She was eating fruits and vegetables and protein, so she was being "healthy." I don't know what upset me

The Beginning

more, my concern for her or my own jealousy. Around that time, my parents accused me of being bulimic. They'd heard someone gagging in the bathroom several nights in a row, so they naturally assumed it was me. At that point, I had never made myself vomit, but no one believed me. Later, we found out it was her. Her stomach acid had corroded the toilet bowl in her bathroom; after my mom saw that, Sissy admitted it. I was mad at Sissy for doing this to me. Even though her choices were about her body and not mine, it felt personal. Seeing her like that made me want to be underweight again. I wanted the compliments about my diet, the concern from my mom. Instead of being rewarded for my recovery, I felt punished for it.

Sissy's recovery was much different from mine. It was less circuitous and more concise. Although she visited Barbara, she did not like her, and she ended up going to see another therapist. Her new therapist believed that her eating disorder was a coping mechanism for feelings about our parents' divorce when we were young. Because my eating disorder didn't have anything to do with that, I didn't understand why hers would. At that point, I didn't realize that eating disorders could be about *anything*. In therapy, instead of journaling her food, Sissy was taught to eat intuitively. At first, she gained weight very quickly. When I reflect on this time, I am still amazed and inspired by her strength and courage. She trusted her therapist. She ate what her body wanted. Eventually, she stopped binge eating and found her normal again. The eating disorder became a thing of the past for her. When I later asked her about how she was able to recover so fully in such a short period of time, she said she remembered what mattered most in her life. Being skinny was not worth losing everything else for her. Unfortunately, recovery was not that straightforward for me. Despite having a system of values, part of my identity was deeply rooted in being thin, and it would be for years to come.

— 2 —

After Anorexia

Throughout junior high school and high school, my body image and eating habits were inconsistent. In seventh and eight grade, I maintained my weight with sufficient caloric intake, but I avoided certain foods without fail. There were good foods and bad foods, clearly delineated in my mind. I later learned that this attempt to eat "perfectly healthy" is sometimes referred to as orthorexia (an unhealthy obsession with healthy eating).

I remember attending a "Disciple Now" retreat in my hometown the summer before eight grade. We stayed at someone's home for a weekend retreat, and each girl brought their favorite snacks. The other girls contributed a spread of potato chips, cookies, and non-diet soda. I brought my low carb protein cereal (which tasted a bit like cardboard), grapes, and Diet Coke. I was careful about everything I ate. I clung to the rules I'd created for myself because I was so afraid of what I would eat or who I would become without them. A part of me was proud; I ate more healthfully than my peers. Another part of me was jealous as I watched them eat. Most of them were thin without ever having thought about calorie counting or restriction.

I continued to pack my lunch for school every day of junior high. I refused to eat the cafeteria food; I had labeled it as off-limits. Still, no matter how hard I tried, I wasn't super skinny anymore. I often felt disappointed in myself, as if I had failed by letting go of my anorexia. When I didn't fit in with the most popular girls in my class, I blamed my weight. When I look back at pictures, I am always saddened, because at that point in my life, I still looked underweight. My body dysmorphia kept me from seeing reality.

My best friend at the time, Tinsley, was very thin and had a very small build. She was also a gymnast, which naturally led to her being a very good cheerleader. As a tiny, strong person, she was the "flyer" in all the cheerleading stunts. I, on the other hand, was a backspot, not strong enough to be a base who held the other girls up, and not small enough to be a flyer. I was so jealous of Tinsley; I longed to be the flyer, the top performer, the center of attention, the fragile girl that others held up. Unfortunately, I spent a lot of my friendship with Tinsley comparing myself to her. We had so much fun together and could talk about anything, but I never told her how jealous I was of her body. Like everyone else in my life, she had no idea that my "recovery" from anorexia was purely physical. I was often trapped in my self hatred, wishing I could be someone else, when all along I had so much to offer my friendships and the world.

When I finally allowed myself to eat the foods I had considered bad for so long, I could not control myself. I started binge eating without knowing that it was pathological. It usually happened late at night, when I was alone. I would raid the pantry and freezer for sweets. Toaster strudels, pop tarts, ice cream, a jar of peanut butter or frosting with a spoon. The eating was automatic, mindless, happening so fast that I could hardly taste the food. When I got to a point where my stomach was full, I kept going. "This is your last time to have these foods," I would tell myself, and then I would eat more. I will never forget the day I walked into my English class, and a classmate of mine (who was also a cheerleader with me) asked me if I was "putting on weight". She meant it as a compliment. She was grinning, sizing up the curves I was developing, but it devastated me. The more devastated I became about the shape my body was taking, the more I wanted foods that were off limits. It was as if my body rebelled against my mind.

My mom noticed these new habits at some point, and she understood. She told me about the times she had eaten an entire box of Krispy Kreme donuts during high school, about how she had gained weight and then felt bad about herself. She told me that her grandmother was horrified about her weight gain, how she'd pointed it out to her mother at Sunday lunch. Then my mom would tell me that she wanted to help me get things "under control" so that I felt good about myself. She signed me up for a gym membership with her. We would "do it together." She wanted to help me be my happiest. At the end of these conversations, I always knew that she wanted me to be thin just as much as I did. I entered into a state of perpetual dieting. I was never the size I wanted to be, but I was also never able to eat normally. I cycled between over eating and under eating.

At family gatherings, for birthdays and holidays, we usually went to my grandmother's house. Such gatherings became a trigger for me because there was so much food, and the celebration was always centered around food. I always wanted more of the food, especially the dessert, but I was also always on a diet. I knew that my mom and grandmother were watching what I put on my plate. I knew that if I ate too much, I'd be disappointing myself, but also my family. When I stuck to my "diet" I would look for positive feedback from my mom, "I did good tonight, right?"

As I gained weight, I began to weigh myself whenever I saw a scale. I thought it would motivate me to eat less, to do "better." My mom had a scale in her bathroom, and I would use it every time I went in there to take a bath in her Jacuzzi bathtub. There was also a scale at my grandmother's house, in her bathroom. I would sneak away from family events, pretending to go pet the dogs, but actually using the scale. If my weight wasn't what I'd hoped, I convinced myself each time, then I could start another diet, a new diet. I could "fix it". I never left my grandmother's bathroom scale feeling less hungry, less food-obsessed, or less insecure. I often felt triggered by the number, and I returned to the dessert table for comfort in the form of seconds or thirds, or at least to scrape the frosting from the cake when no one was looking.

I developed bulimia. I cannot recall the first time that I made myself throw up, but I think it was at a family gathering. After eating past fullness, I felt terrible, physically and emotionally. It felt like the only solution. I could eat whatever I wanted on a holiday and then go to the bathroom and get rid of it. In some ways, I felt like it didn't count if it wasn't my bathroom, like it wasn't really happening. I always knew it was bad for my health. I always knew it was disrespectful to do it in someone else's bathroom. I always knew that my family wouldn't approve if they found out. I just couldn't keep myself from doing it, not when I had already eaten too much, not when I thought about how long it would take my body to digest all that food and feel "good" again, and not when I thought about the number on the scale.

I would wait until it seemed like no one would miss me. I would sneak into the bathroom, lock the door, and turn on the faucet. I would roll up my sleeves and pull back my hair. I didn't need to stick anything down my throat, not when I was so full already. All I had to do was vomit. It was like a reflex, and once I got started, I could gag and keep going. In time, I learned that there were certain foods that were easier to throw up than others, certain foods that didn't hurt my throat as much. Afterwards, I would flush the toilet, rinse out my mouth, and assess myself in the mirror. I would hide all the evidence, put on a fake smile, and rejoin the party.

On one of these occasions, after weighing myself and feeling particularly hopeless, my friend John came to visit me. He was my first best friend who was not a girl. We would drive around for hours in his old pick up truck listening to punk rock and emo music from his ipod. He called me his little sister, and it felt like we could talk about anything. I had never told him about my bulimia; I didn't believe I was bulimic anyway. John pulled his truck into my grandmother's driveway to come say hello to me on a Saturday when my family was spending the day there, having a cookout. I didn't expect him to come visit me that day. He hugged me as his usual greeting, and I kept my left arm close down to my side. He could tell I was hiding something. And then he saw it. He grabbed my hand and turned my arm over to look at the underside of my left wrist. "Did you cut yourself?" he asked with a look of concern and fear on his face.

"No, not really. It's nothing," I said, looking away. I had carved three large capital letters onto my left wrist using a safety pin. There was no bleeding. They were "just scratches," I told him. It was a reminder to myself of what I was going to become if I didn't do a better job with my diet.

"Maggie, you are not fat. You are beautiful." I should have believed him, but all that went through my mind was, "of course you have to say that." Instead I thanked him. I teared up. I promised him I wouldn't do it again. John and I didn't stay close after high school. It's weird to realize that someone who lifted you up after seeing the darkest part of you could just be an old friend. I wondered if I scared him away. Did he realize that day that I was more superficial than he would ever be?

So much of high school, my joy for life overshadowed my desire to be thinner. In some ways, I was strong enough to know who I was and what mattered to me. I quit cheerleading and joined the debate team instead. I found my greatest friends in high school on the debate and forensics (competitive theatre) teams. Yet I continued to focus on my weight. I skipped lunch and drank diet soda instead. I cut out pictures of skinny swimsuit and lingerie models from magazines and hung them on my bedroom wall for inspiration. How surprising it would have been to all of my high school friends to know that I would have traded my intelligence to look like a Victoria's Secret model! How embarrassing it would have been for me to admit to someone that I didn't have the body I wanted and that I couldn't get it no matter how hard I tried! That part of my life was hidden from everyone.

America's Junior Miss (now known as Distinguished Young Women) was a scholarship pageant for high school juniors created in 1958. Contestants were judged in the categories of interview, scholastics, talent, fitness, and self-expression (which involved parading around the stage in an evening gown). I do not intend to belittle people who participate in pageants. I do believe some pageants help women achieve their goals, form relationships with other amazing women, and develop platforms for sharing for their passions. However, I realize now that Junior Miss had a negative impact on me by fueling my eating disorder.

    I knew that I would do very well in Junior Miss if I chose to participate. I had a good talent (I was very skilled at piano), scholastic prowess, and interview skills due to my experience with public speaking. All I had to work on were fitness and beauty. "If you lost ten pounds you would be a knock-out," my mother would say. This sentence echoed in my head every time I looked in the mirror. It was an expensive pageant and would cost at least a couple thousand dollars, so I understand why Mama wanted me to fully commit to it. No one has ever won a pageant, even a scholarship pageant, without being both thin *and* fit. There was an understanding between me Mama that I would lose weight to reach my full potential and have a chance at winning the pageant. If we were going to spend so much time and money on Junior Miss, I would give it my all.

    In the midst of my preparations for the pageant, I received the opportunity to serve as a United States House of Representatives Page. Even though I had already lost ten pounds, learned a new piece on the piano, and picked out an evening gown, I decided not to do Junior Miss. Instead, I spent an entire semester in Washington, D.C. My time as a page was one of the best in my life. I "found myself" in many ways, and I made some of the deepest friendships I've ever had, including my friendship with Amy. She and I became inseparable immediately. We were both outgoing with positive outlooks on life, liked to make others laugh, and had the same sense of humor. We were also both Christians and came from Southern families; our morals and upbringing were similar. Amy was tall and athletic, and she was secure in her own skin. She once told me that her mother wanted her to "watch her weight," but that she knew that her natural body was not "skinny" and that she was taking good care of herself.

    It was the first time in my life (at least since childhood) that I allowed myself to eat whatever I wanted. I regularly consumed the Capitol building's fried chicken strips, french fries, tuna fish sandwiches, and frozen yogurt bar, as well as twinkies from the dorm vending machine. Amy and I sometimes took some of the leftover gigantic muffins from the breakfast room and ate them for dessert. I gained weight. I'm not sure how much because I did not have a scale, nor did I actively desire to know my weight. However, for some reason, it didn't feel important. Surrounded by peers from around the country who were equally passionate about their futures, for the first time in my life, I felt loved and celebrated simply for being *Maggie*. Neither my weight nor my appearance had anything to do with it.

At the end of the semester, there was a "graduation" ceremony. I was sad to leave but also somewhat nervous to see my family and to return home to my friends. I worried that everyone would notice my weight gain. I suppose it was other people's reactions to my weight gain that worried me more than the weight gain itself. After our initial greeting, I asked my mom if she could tell I'd gained weight, and she said that she could. She reassured me by saying it would be easy for me to "get back on track" before it was "too late" and other people noticed too. At the end of my time as a page, I went back to Mississippi, heartbroken to leave the friends who made me realize I was enough, and I started dieting again.

— 3 —

College, Cancer, and Control

MY EXPERIENCE AT RHODES College was much like my experience as a page. I found a world where my natural personality traits and talents were celebrated. This did not mean that my concerns about weight were gone, however. I spent the summer leading up to college dieting. I wanted to look my best for sorority recruitment or "rush." My mother even told me that one of her friends had seen my Facebook pictures and commented that I looked thin; I could tell she was proud of me for this. Learning to eat on the meal plan at college was somewhat overwhelming because the cafeteria was an all-you-can-eat buffet. I began to gain weight and was devastated when my clothes weren't fitting as well. I also frequently compared my body to the bodies of other girls my age. I did not drink alcohol when I was under the legal age, but when college was stressful, I sometimes turned to food. I kept a box of Reese's Puffs cereal in my dorm room and often ate late at night.

After a housekeeper in our dormitory commented to me in passing that I was "getting thick, pretty thighs," which she clearly meant as a compliment, I had a meltdown. It was as if I'd been trying not to think about my size and had told myself I was the same as when I started college. I cried to my suite-mate and best friend, Sasha, about how I felt about my body. She simply listened to me, let me lay next to her in her bed, and reminded me of all the good things I was that didn't have anything to do with my weight or my appearance. She helped me to remember why I was enough.

Soon after this episode, I learned that my college had free counseling and decided to give it a try. At that point, I didn't go to therapy because I wanted to lose weight or stop a certain habit; I wanted to get help with my body image, to make it less important to me. It was the right motivation. I saw a therapist who was in the process of becoming certified. Emma had a nose ring and long blonde hair, and she smelled like cigarette smoke (I did see her smoking outside on campus a few times). Her strategy was to dig deeper into my past to help me understand why I had such an issue with my body when I was a healthy weight. This was new for me; Barbara never dug into my past, she just taught me what to do next. During my most memorable and helpful session with Emma, she used a technique called "chairing." I sat facing an empty chair and pretended that the childhood version of myself, Little Maggie, was in front of me. I spoke to Little Maggie and apologized for being so angry at her for simply being herself. I apologized for all the times I had punished her for being imperfect, because she didn't deserve it. I then switched chairs and pretended to be Little Maggie, speaking to my present self. Little Maggie expressed just how difficult it had been for her to receive so much criticism and anger, how she had only wanted to be happy and free, how she knew she had done nothing wrong; then she forgave me. As strange as this experience was, it allowed me to realize that the years of punishing myself and my body for being imperfect were harmful.

At the end of my freshman year of college, I was diagnosed with Ewing sarcoma, a rare type of childhood bone cancer. I was forced to take a year off from my beloved college due to the severe side effects of my high dose chemotherapy. Immediately after my diagnosis, I was in shock. For several weeks, I did not think about my weight or my body or my diet at all. I was so afraid that I was going to die that the size of my body was irrelevant. Most of the things I cared about in life, including my future career, began to seem trivial. As I waited for biopsy results, I ate Domino's pizza dipped in ranch dressing, freely and without judgment. I did not feel guilty for eating, and I stopped when I was full without even trying. It was as if the moment I stopped caring about how fat or skinny I was, my appetite followed suit.

My year of cancer treatment was the hardest year of my life so far. My life and identity were turned upside down. I wish I could tell you that I maintained perspective and continued to feel like my body size was irrelevant throughout my treatment, but this would be a lie. I began to lose weight from the chemotherapy, which gave me intractable nausea and vomiting. For three to six days at a time (depending on which drug I was getting), I was admitted to the hospital. As soon as the drug infusions began, so did the nausea. My vomiting quickly turned to dry heaving as my stomach remained empty for my entire stay. In the midst of crippling nausea, which rarely improved with the anti nausea medications, I often felt hunger pains, but I wouldn't eat. Nothing tasted the way it was supposed to taste, and the smell of food made the nausea worse. In a somewhat sedated state due to the IV lorazepam (the only anti nausea drug I was allowed to take due to an abnormal heart rhythm that these drugs make worse), I would tell my mother what I wanted to eat when I got out of chemo. I envisioned entire meals at a variety of my favorite restaurants. By the end of the chemo cycle, my body was weak and a few pounds lighter. I would go back to our nearby apartment and begin to heal until I was due to the next treatment, two and a half weeks later.

I visited the clinic at least twice a week between my hospital admissions. A nurse drew my blood for labs and recorded my vital signs, including my weight in kilograms. At the beginning of that year, seeing my weight didn't bother me. The number was slowly falling, which made sense. However, as my weight continued to fall, my doctor was concerned for my health and said I would need a feeding tube if I didn't stop losing weight. I needed the nutrition for my body to heal, and I had been a healthy weight at the beginning of my treatment. My job, then, was to catch up on my eating in between each chemotherapy session. Although I enjoyed having the chance to eat whatever I wanted and view it as an achievement, I felt conflicted because I'd begun to enjoy the weight loss. I had quickly become the thinnest I'd been in years, and even though I was hairless with dark circles under my eyes, I thought I looked better at my new weight. I was given weight goals; if I didn't gain a kilogram over the long weekend, then I would have to get the tube. The thought of having tube feeds upset me because I didn't want a long tube going from my nose into my stomach at all times, but I also did not want to get my calories from liquid food supplements when I could be eating really good foods. Above all else, I also didn't want to gain back any weight. I wanted to maintain my weight loss because I liked the results.

Even after my doctor had set a goal for me to gain weight, when I saw my weight had increased, I felt ashamed and disappointed. Seeing the higher numbers on the scale upset me so much that I began asking nurses to do blind weights. I would face away from the scale while they wrote down my weight. The system wasn't perfect, though. Nurses were well meaning but often forgot and said my weight aloud. One nurse once said to me, "You look so great! I can tell you've gained weight!" She was happy for me and thought I looked healthier, but I cried about it later that day. How surprising it was that I cared so much about my weight in the midst of battling cancer! I felt guilty about this, but the guilt didn't make me care less.

Looking back, I wonder if I focused so much on my weight because it was one of the few things I could control during that year. I could not control my blood counts, the side effects of my chemotherapy, or my cancer's response to treatment; my life was not in my hands. However, I could control my weight, and if I had to gain weight, I was not going to gain a pound more than I had to. Being a cancer patient became my identity, and somewhere along the way, that identity became entangled with being skinny.

This became a problem when my treatment came to an end. While my body had become the means through which I could remain alive and in the world, something to cherish, it also felt separate from me. Through chemotherapy, I'd had to punish it over and over again; the only way for me to survive was to hurt my body. This left me feeling separate from my body rather than

College, Cancer, and Control

united. Although I was ecstatic to become cured of cancer and to go back to college afterwards, it was difficult to adjust back to normal life. Living in a hospital, under constant surveillance by my doctors and nurses, felt so safe. No one cared what I was wearing, I stopped using makeup (it doesn't make sense when you don't have eyelashes and eyebrows), and I wore glasses instead of contacts every day. The biggest change I had to endure was leaving a world where love and family meant everything, where the point of being alive was to be with loved ones, where nothing was taken for granted. I had spent so much uninterrupted quality time with my mom and my sisters, and that special time in our lives had come to an end.

My return to college was filled with excitement. It was such a happy time for me. It was filled with gratitude. I had a new lease on life, as they say. I was excited to wake up each day. I was relieved to be well. I thanked God every day for my life. I threw myself into my academics, back in my element, at last. I realized I'd been deprived from studying the way that I longed to study while I had been in cancer treatment. I got involved with friendships and spent hours giggling with my girlfriends. I started thinking about boys and dating again. In some ways I got to relive my freshman year of college. I had sat out an entire year, so I joined the sophomore class that would have been the class behind me. I felt more confident in my appearance because I could wear all the clothes I'd always wanted to wear but hadn't always flattered me at my old weight. I had very short hair and experimented with it all the time, which was fun. I had so much motivation behind my career goals because I didn't simply want to be a doctor; I wanted to be a doctor for kids with cancer. I savored my time in classes and with friends because I had missed all of it so much. I transitioned from being a cancer patient to a "new and improved" version of myself. That new version also lived life to the fullest, took more risks, made more friends, and tried more new things.

Slowly, some of the weight I had lost started to return. Without a five day chemotherapy session every few weeks, my appetite and my energy level skyrocketed. I became stronger with more muscle tone. My hip bones and collar bones became less protuberant. My body became a little softer, my breasts a little fuller. All of these should have been good things, and I knew that they were a sign of health, but I was terrified. I had not done this on purpose. I had not given my body permission to gain weight. I associated weight gain with the old Maggie, the one who was ungrateful for life, who was held back by her insecurities and her lack of perspective, who got cancer in the first place. Weighing more would change my identity yet again. If not the cancer patient, and not the new and improved Maggie, then who would I be? As soon as I started to worry about my weight again, my eating patterns became unhealthier. I started to binge eat again, which caused me to worry about my weight more, which caused me to restrict more, which caused me to binge eat more. I was back in a vicious cycle. With every diet, I thought that I was protecting myself from becoming overweight, from ballooning out. I thought that I was helping myself. I did not realize that I was hurting myself more, training my brain to be deprived.

I had previously seen a therapist, Violet, for anxiety and depression while I was going through cancer treatment. I continued to see her after I returned to school to help me with the transition back to normal life. When I met with her, I had so much guilt about my unhappiness. I was alive and well, thriving in college academically and socially, but I was terrified of gaining weight. I felt like a bad person for caring about my weight when I was so lucky to be alive. Violet didn't know how to coach me regarding my eating habits, but she did teach me that it was "okay" for me to have problems that weren't cancer. It was a good thing that cancer wasn't the main thing on my mind. It was a sign that I was becoming my normal self again if this mattered to me. I had to learn to accept the fact that my feelings about my body weren't my fault. They weren't there because I was a bad or ungrateful person. She taught me that hating myself for caring about my weight was not going to make me feel any better.

During junior year of college, the bulimia returned. I wasn't just purging at family holidays. It was every time I had a big meal, sometimes several nights out of the week. My roommates were worried about me. I felt horrible about it. I felt guilty and depressed every time it happened because I knew it was unhealthy. I believed I wasn't going to be able to stop bingeing and purging until I lost some weight. I felt unattractive and unhealthy at my weight, and this made me feel depressed. My solution for my depression was weight loss.

The counselor I saw this time, Pat, did not specialize in eating disorders. She primarily helped people with anxiety and depression. Her advice to me was not unique. She encouraged me to focus on things other than my weight. She referred me to a psychiatrist so that I could restart an SSRI for depression. She encouraged me to think about food in terms of health instead of weight. She gave me tips for redirecting myself when I felt triggered to binge or purge. All of these things were good, but they weren't enough. They were like bandaids instead of the surgery I needed. It was detrimental, however, when Pat sent me to a local eating disorder support group.

We sat in a circle of chairs, looking at one another as we shared stories, like what I'd seen in the movies about Alcoholics Anonymous meetings. I spent the entire time comparing myself to other people in the group. Was I as skinny as that person? Was my problem as bad as theirs? One group member even shared tips about how to vomit without getting cavities. There was another girl in the group whom I recognized from my college, Ivy, and she shared stories about all of the times she would binge and purge while on the job as a restaurant waitress. Every time I ran into Ivy on campus, we smiled at one another awkwardly, and I envisioned her hunched over a toilet with her finger down the back of her throat. Days after the support group meeting, voices echoed in my mind, encouraging me to try harder at weight loss, to fully commit to my problem, to prove myself to the group. I knew that these voices were better left ignored, so I did not return to the support group.

The day that I told my now-husband, Drew, about my long term struggle with my weight was a day that was monumental for our relationship. We had been dating for a little over a year, but there were still some things he didn't know about me, mostly the bad parts. That morning, after several days of eating only vegetables, I weighed myself for the first time in a while, and the number had actually gone up instead of down. I was so upset that I spent the rest of the afternoon crying in bed. Drew came by my dorm room to visit me when I wasn't expecting it.

He wanted to know what was wrong, and I didn't want to lie to him. I was nervous about what he might think. He was the opposite of superficial, and I didn't want him to think that I was superficial. I told him about the eating disorder I'd had as a teenager, how after all this time I still felt very upset when I wasn't the weight I wanted to be. His reaction was love-filled. He looked at me with understanding rather than judgment. He told me that he loved me for reasons other than my looks, that I was beautiful to him, and that he had never noticed my size. He opened up to me in return and told me that he also had a problem he sometimes struggled with. He laid beside me in my twin-sized bed and held me until I didn't feel the need to cry anymore. I fell in love with him again that day. He became my accountability partner. With Drew around, I did not want to throw up anymore, and for a long time I didn't.

My relationship with my body became even more complicated when I was diagnosed with infertility. I knew something was off when I started having hot flashes and fatigue at the end of my junior year. The sensations of menopause were familiar because my period had been suppressed during chemo by a medication called depot-lupron, which forced my ovaries to go into menopause temporarily in an effort to prevent infertility. I was referred to a gynecologist for labs. My follicular stimulating hormone and luteinizing hormone were incredibly high, and my estrogen very low. This indicated that my brain was making extra signaling hormones to try to stimulate my ovaries, which were not working to produce estrogen. Follow up testing of my anti-mullerian hormone showed it to be extremely low at <.1 (the level for a fertile woman is 1.0–4.0), which meant that I had very little follicular reserve. The final step was an ovarian ultrasound in an attempt to identify ovarian follicles. The doctor only visualized two follicles in total (normal would have been close to twenty). All of this information meant that my ovaries had been damaged from chemo and were behaving as if they belonged to a seventy year-old woman. The gynecologist told me my results with great care; I could tell she was sad for me.

I, on the other hand, was not sad. I reminded myself that I was lucky to be alive and did not shed a single tear. I told Drew about the results later that day, and he told me that it didn't change the way he felt about our future together, even if that meant we had to adopt a baby. While I am grateful for my ability to receive this news with grace, I wonder if I was actually just in denial about it. Years would pass before I ever allowed myself to cry about my infertility. I was *alive,* for God's sake. I thought that should be enough. As time passed, though, a very quiet anger began to build inside of me. I was angry at my body for its weakness, for being the one in ten percent of women who had infertility from the chemotherapy I had received. Once again, my body had betrayed me and had become my enemy. If I could have viewed my body as a home for a future baby, as a vessel for love, then I think it would have been easier to love it.

In the spring of senior year, I began to have anxiety about graduation, going to medical school, and moving away from Drew. I told myself that I would feel better about everything if I lost weight. I began waking up early to go to the gym for thirty minutes of cardio each morning. I replaced my buffet breakfasts with low carb protein shakes. At lunch and dinner, I ate mostly salad, but I told myself I could have whatever I wanted, so I filled up my tray with lots of options and threw most of it away. By allowing myself to pretend I was eating whatever I wanted, I didn't feel left out. As I went to bed each night, I felt my stomach rumble, and although I did not have the willpower to ignore the stomach pains, I found that sucking on small sour candies as I fell asleep helped dull the hunger. In the afternoons, when I was tired, instead of pushing through my studying by having a coffee and a snack, I would nap. Napping kept me from eating more and brought me closer to the next meal, for which I was always hungry.

Skinny or Not, Here I Come

Throughout this regimen, I weighed myself obsessively, every morning as soon as I woke up. I no longer considered myself as having disordered eating; I was just really good at being thin. I felt more confident about my appearance, and this allowed me to feel some sense of reassurance about the future. In the month leading up to graduation, my mom came to visit and took me shopping. We went to my favorite store, *Free People,* and I tried on lots of dresses. Many of their clothes have always been too revealing or too tight for me. On this occasion, everything fit perfectly. In one dress, the size 4 was loose, and the size 2 was perfect. I was thrilled; I had never been a size 2 before. When we left the store, my mom told me that I looked amazing but that I didn't need to lose any more weight. I could tell that she was slightly concerned, but I also wondered if she was proud of me for being thin. I told her that I was eating, and I was, but only a few bites at each meal.

Soon after this, Drew and I had lunch together. When he had finished eating, he watched me pick at my food for a while and then told me he was worried about my eating disorder. He said that his dad was worried too, that his dad had noticed my weight loss and had "warned him to be careful" about being serious with someone who had an eating disorder. I reassured Drew that I was not trying to lose any more weight. He asked me to take another bite of my chicken, and I did. I was partially flattered that people were noticing how skinny I was and partially offended that Drew's dad had given him a warning. However, I wasn't worried about myself: I was proud of myself. The only thing I was worried about was losing control of my eating again; I felt like I was walking the edge of a cliff and might fall off and begin a cycle of binge eating at any moment. I had to stay in control in order to be happy, I told myself.

— 4 —

Low Points at Low Weights

WHEN I STARTED MEDICAL school, I was perfectly primed for the eating disorder. At the end of college, I had gotten a taste of what it was like to be my ideal weight, and I wanted to stay that way. I was also living away from family and away from anyone I knew, with a roommate who was also always on a diet. Drew and I were long distance, and I only saw him every few weeks for weekend visits. To top it all off, medical school was hard; I had to study harder than ever before in order to simply be average in my class.

My first moments of nearly every day consisted of getting out of bed, using the bathroom, stripping off my pajamas, and stepping on the scale. If I couldn't do this ritual, I felt anxious and insecure. If I couldn't see a number on the scale, then the mirror convinced me that I had gained weight. Seeing the number on the scale defined my day. If the number was lower than the day before, that was a good day. If it was higher, even if it was still within a small range, it was a bad day. No matter what the number was, I went to the gym afterwards. My weight oscillated within a range of about twelve pounds over the four years of medical school, depending on how "successful" I had been with my dieting. When a diet failed, it often ended in an episode of bingeing, and sometimes purging.

After one episode of bingeing and purging, I felt like I had hit rock bottom. I called a friend for advice. Lacey had been one of my childhood babysitters, and she had also struggled with an eating disorder. She had overcome this eating disorder and made a career out of health and wellness coaching as well as cooking healthy foods. Not only did she seem like she was always eating, her bikini pictures on Instagram demonstrated that she was very skinny with perfectly defined eight-pack abs. I wanted to find what she had found. Because I considered her to be healed from her eating disorder and able to eat well and stay thin, I trusted her. I called her several times and began to follow her instructions.

Lacey gave me a new set of rules that I tried to live by. She confided in me that she, too, had episodes of bingeing and purging. "I would eat so much that I *had* to throw up." It didn't sound like a choice. I gave myself permission to think of it in this way. Purging was not a choice after binge eating, it was just what *had to be done*. I asked Lacey if I should weigh myself every day. She responded, "Yes, it's good to be able to point a finger on the problem."

This convinced me that people who had issues with food were actually better off weighing themselves daily. It convinced me that I needed to keep going with this. Her mantra was "consistency is key," and I found myself repeating it inside my head whenever I had cravings or whenever my weight wasn't what I had hoped it would be. A while later, when I consulted her for advice with a text that said, "I want to lose five pounds," she responded with, "stop eating carbs after noon, and stay consistent."

Daily weights helped to hold me accountable to my diet, so I bought a small digital scale that I could pack in my luggage and take with me when I visit Drew, who had become my fiance. My diets would go well when I was alone but fell apart when I visited him. We went out to dinner, sipped on wine at vineyards, and bought popcorn at the movie theater. He loved treating me to frozen yogurt; it was our tradition from college. I would indulge and then gain back the few pounds I'd lost the week before. On the long drive back from Kansas City to Rochester, I would berate myself for six hours and plan the next diet. I felt incredibly lonely, having Drew ripped away from me. I felt angry with myself. I would either start my diet at that point or I would allow myself one more night to binge eat on whatever I wanted. Perhaps it was easier for me to focus on my weight than my emotions. It was something I could manipulate and change, rather than the fact that I was in love with someone who I only saw once every few weeks. Perhaps it was a coping mechanism, a return to familiar feelings of self-hatred and self-deprecation rather than grieving about something that would only get better once I was in the same place as Drew, which was dependent on where I matched for residency.

A binge was always in the setting of deprivation, either physical or mental. If I hadn't been dieting, I had been telling myself that the eating I was doing was wrong and only temporary. If I actually ate without inhibitions, then guilt, self-hatred, and fear would follow. It was an irrational but unstoppable fear that my body would continue to grow until I was *stuck there.* "Stop while you're ahead," I would tell myself. My mother's words would echo in my mind, "Right now you're the only one that knows. Stop before it's too late, before people can notice a difference." Holidays were the most difficult times for me. I couldn't hold back because it was the one time I justified eating everything I "wanted." The problem was, I wanted *everything.* Holidays, in this way, were exhausting for me. They did not feel restful, perhaps because of the dread that followed me throughout each day, dread of the aftermath. There was usually purging as well. I would eat until I was physically ill, promising myself that I would start an effective diet "tomorrow" and eating way more than I would have without the diet hanging over my head. The morning after a binge, I would feel physically and emotionally broken. I would feel trapped. I could not resist the urge to weigh myself. I felt the number gave me a sense of reality, something tangible to cling to, and an indicator of just how "far gone" I was from binge eating. But the number was a punishment. Every time I looked at the number on the scale, I reminded myself of how I had "failed" to reach a goal I had set for myself.

I truly believed that this goal was important work in my life because I had a problem with overeating. To address this problem, I had to constantly work at it. I believed that I was incapable of happiness unless I was the body type I wanted to be. I also believed that if I stopped trying to diet, I would gain weight without any end point. For these reasons, I relentlessly chugged forward, starving myself again and again in order to maintain my weight and therefore my happiness. Something shifted within me the winter of my second year of medical school. It was the end of another vacation, which meant the end of my time with Drew and family for a long while. It also meant the aftermath of weeks of binge eating. Despite the fact that my wedding was approaching, I felt horrible about myself. I wondered if it was common to have this much anxiety leading up to my wedding, not about the planning, but about myself. I wondered how I could feel so bad about myself as I prepared to marry the most amazing person I'd ever met.

On a whim, I sent an email to a psychologist and asked her if we could meet for a session. She was an eating disorder expert and had given a lecture to our class. She didn't have any openings for new patients, but she agreed to see me for a session and give me a referral to someone in her group. I sat down in her office and began to explain my struggle. She was beautiful. I had seen her at the grocery store the week before, buying pasta and pesto sauce. I had looked at her and thought, "there is no way she eats that stuff; it must be for her family." She was compassionate and honest, and she told me that she thought I had an active eating disorder. She said I would stop binge eating only when I stopped dieting, that my solution was actually to stop dieting. Later that day, while on the phone with my mom, I told her that I was tired of dieting and was considering allowing my body to be its natural size.

"I just want more than anything for you to be happy on your wedding day," she responded. "We are spending so much money on this day, and I know that you won't enjoy it if you're not the weight you want to be." I am sad that she couldn't help me stand up for myself in that moment, that she didn't want me to fight for my happiness in the setting of weight gain, to make my wedding about so much more than what I looked like. I am sad that I didn't tell her that I wanted or needed that support from her. I just wasn't there yet, so I threw away the glimmer of hope that my psychology session had planted in me, and I frequently reminded myself that losing weight was the only way I could possibly enjoy my wedding day.

Low Points at Low Weights

The diet I embarked upon next was very similar to the one senior year of college. As I studied for a board exam, I skipped meals and only ate when I felt dizzy or ravenous, at which point it was mostly vegetables. I often sucked on candy and drank diet soda in ridiculous proportions to quell my hunger. I began to experience episodes of hypoglycemia, with my heart racing and palms sweating, usually after eating nothing all day and then eating a piece of candy. I also began to abuse laxatives during this time, giving myself bowel clean outs because my weight was at its lowest right after my bowel movements. I somehow managed to study for one of the hardest exams of my life while barely eating. I got back down to my goal weight and maintained it until the wedding.

It breaks my heart to admit the next part. On the day of my wedding, I stepped into my wedding dress, and it fit perfectly. It fit like a glove, which is usually what every bride prays for, but I had hoped it would be a little loose after all my hard work. Standing alone with my mom and looking in the mirror as I prepared for me and Drew to have our "first look," I cried because I thought I looked fat. After endless dieting, the most amazing dress, and perfect hair and makeup, I still wasn't skinny or pretty enough for my inner critic. Mama reassured me, told me how beautiful I looked, and helped me to focus my attention on what the day was really about. When I saw Drew, I completely forgot about how I looked. Although the moments that I spent unhappy on my wedding day were few, I am sad that they existed at all. My eating disorder was getting in the way of my life.

Although I packed my small portable scale for the honeymoon, I chose not to use it in Hawaii. I didn't want my time with Drew to be tainted by the unavoidable weight fluctuations that would happen on vacation. I suppose it was a small act of love that I gave myself. At the end of our honeymoon, we returned to our respective homes six hours apart, with still two years of graduate school to go. I cried most of the way back, devastated to leave him again. Not only was he my soulmate; he also protected me from dieting. I knew I would go back to it yet again.

Skinny or Not, Here I Come

During this time, I couldn't miss a day of working out. I was proud of myself at the time. Drew encouraged me to take a day off once in a while, but I could rarely do it. I felt like my day wasn't a productive one if I didn't work out. I convinced myself that this was a sign of health consciousness. There were even a few times when I went to the gym at 4:00 a.m. because I had to go to the airport for an early flight. I remember a lady who was always at the gym on a treadmill alongside mine. She seemed to go around 5:30 a.m. each day. I looked at her with a mixture of admiration and disgust. She had long, thin hair and pale skin. She was emaciated, but she would run and run and sweat longer than I would. I wanted her to take a break. Maybe I saw some of myself in her. Maybe I recognized what she was doing because I did it too, I just didn't look like it on the outside.

My workouts were not only compulsive; they were often brutal. In my right leg, I have a total knee and tibia prosthesis. Low impact exercise is recommended. I never have learned to run well with this leg, and I was told not to try. I found that walking on the treadmill at a twenty percent incline made for a very tiring workout, and according to the calorimeter, burned about five hundred calories in thirty minutes. I looked ridiculous. Several times, fitness instructors at the gym tried to intervene and tell me that the incline I was walking on was not good for my body. I always ended up crying because I felt like it was the only way I could burn the calories I wanted to burn. I developed calluses on the pads of my hands from gripping the handles of the treadmill so tightly. I got through these workouts because I allowed myself to watch "trashy" reality television whenever I was at the gym. I found these shows motivating because all of the women were very thin and perfectly styled. Watching them on the treadmill was as if I was walking towards my goal: looking more like them. I told myself that the morals and values conveyed on these shows were not my own, but that wasn't completely true. I had come to value being thin and pretty more than my health.

At my lowest weight in medical school, I began to struggle with anxiety and depression, which turned into panic disorder. For a long time, I blamed my panic attacks on other things. I was in a long distance marriage, I lived alone, and when I wasn't on clinical rotations, I was studying. I also didn't have as many good friends in medical school as I'd had in college. I felt excluded by most of my classmates and assumed they didn't like me because I wasn't invited to many of their gatherings. Looking back, I realize that it was I who avoided them to begin with. I had been included at the beginning of medical school, but I stopped going to many social events because I told myself I needed to study or go to the gym instead. I also avoided going to dinner or parties sometimes because I didn't want to be around the "temptation" of food and wine; if I stayed at home, I could stick to my diet.

When I first started having panic attacks, I was convinced that I had a cardiac arrhythmia or a neurological disease (I was on my neurology rotation at that time). One moment, I would feel fine, and the next I would feel dizzy, nauseated, and sweaty, with my heart racing and my fingers and toes tingling. In addition to the physical symptoms, I felt overwhelmed by fear each time it happened. I saw a cardiologist and had a Holter monitor placed for 48 hours to assess my heart rhythm. Apart from a few episodes of tachycardia (my heart racing), it was normal. My primary care doctor obtained labs to check my thyroid and kidney function (I was at high risk of these issues due to my chemotherapy). Everything was normal, so I knew that it had to be anxiety. Still, it was debilitating. I didn't want to leave my apartment because I was afraid it would happen again. The more I feared the episodes, the more they happened. The more they happened, the more I feared that I would never be able to get rid of them.

I went to see a psychiatrist who knew about my eating disorder history. After hearing my symptoms, he diagnosed me with panic disorder. He put me back on an SSRI (I had weaned off of my long term medication months earlier). He scheduled frequent check ups and had me stand on the scale at each appointment. He once said, "be careful, because being malnourished or underweight can make anxiety worse." I told him I was eating "plenty of food" and did not want to lose any more weight, and he believed me.

Skinny or Not, Here I Come

The thing is, I was being honest. I wasn't lying to him. I completely believed I was eating enough at that time. I believed I was a healthy weight because I was at my goal weight. I believed I was taking care of myself. I sometimes even concluded that my anxiety was a manifestation of my mind having nothing to focus on because I was at my ideal weight. For a short time, the best part of my day was seeing the number on the scale. That was my one moment of reprieve. That was the only break I had from the panic. I started to become nauseated every time I ate, so the anxiety propagated my eating disorder. It was a vicious cycle.

Looking back, I think that some of my earlier episodes of "panic," which led to anxiety and then propagated panic disorder, were actually symptoms of malnourishment. It took several months for the antidepressant to "kick in" and for the anxiety to start improving. I think the medication helped my appetite more than anything else, and in turn, that helped everything else. I also had to learn to stop being so afraid of the panic attacks. The anticipation of a panic attack alone was enough to trigger one, and the worry that I would never be "back to normal" made me feel hopeless and terrified. My new therapist, Kristy, taught me how to utilize intentional hyperventilation as a technique during panic attacks. It helped me to feel in control of my physical symptoms and was a way of saying "bring it on" to the panic. I suppose I will never know how much the panic attacks were related to my weight, but I do know that when I gained some weight back, they eventually went away.

When the anxiety dissipated, the eating disorder returned. I met with Kristy when I felt overwhelmed by the roller coaster I was on with feelings about my weight. She was the first therapist to ask me about my values. She gave me an assignment after our first meeting. I had to write down "what I stood for." Kristy wanted to know where (or where else) I found my identity.

> I stand for love and compassion towards others, for understanding and acceptance. I am comfortable with uncertainties when it comes to my faith. I am comfortable with diversity despite my Southern Mississippi

upbringing. I have felt at home in Hindu temples and Indian buffets, in European Cathedrals filled with relics, in Buddhist meditation workshops, and in labyrinths and prayer gardens. I have felt at peace in yoga sessions and in nature, in art galleries and nursing homes. I have been able to find God and hope in the midst of children dying of cancer and as I walked the line between life and death. I am able to sit next to the sick and the dying and feel their sorrow with them as I help them to feel less alone on their journeys. I am able to make meaningful connections on every journey I take and never exit an airplane without a new friend, whether I know their names or not. I am courageous; I take leaps of faith because I know that failure is easier than never reaching for my goals. I feel at home when I am caring for others- physically but especially emotionally. I feel at peace when I am surrounded by people, these magical beings filled with the gift of love. I believe that love is the most beautiful and pure thing in life, and that love is evidence of God and evidence of an afterlife of some kind. I love to laugh and make others laugh and was once recruited by an entertainment agent to perform stand-up-comedy. I love cooking without recipes so I can add whatever feels right in the moment. I love playing the piano, but only when it's songs I write because then I can play what I'm feeling. I love to do arts and crafts, even though they never look like what I set out to create. I love dogs- their innocence and trust and willingness to love completely without judging. I love the feeling I get when I am watching a horror movie and have no clue what will scare me next. I love to dance with my husband, who is also my best friend in the world. I love flowers and gardens and would like to build my own fairy garden. And none of this—none of who I am or who or what I love—is reflected in the way I feel about my body or the things I have done with food. My relationship with my body and food is cold. It is filled with hatred and guilt. It is built of rigidity and rules. It is black and white, all or none, good or bad. It is a number on a scale or a size in a pair of jeans. It is about comparisons and competition, about winning or losing, but I can never win. That eating disorder part of me is not understanding or compassionate; it is judgmental and critical. It does not love anyone or anything except control. It hates laughter and social occasions. It is afraid of love or hope or taking any risks at all. It is lonely and afraid, but instead of reaching out for help, it pretends that it can control the whole world by the way it eats. My eating disorder believes that people should be punished—that I should be punished—for imperfection. I realize that even after 12 years, there are two parts to me. The eating disorder is still there, expressing her thoughts and opinions and punishing me whenever I choose to listen. I no longer want to make room for her inside of me. I want to be all the things that I value and all the things that I truly am. I want to learn to eat with compassion for myself. I want to learn to bathe my body and exercise and get dressed in ways that are gentle and loving and not judgmental and fueled by hate or shame. And once I am free, I want to teach others to be free, too.

During our time together, Kristy helped me to tap into the reality that being thin was a distraction from who I really was and who I wanted to become. She helped me to realize that I wasn't actually binge eating many of the times I thought I was; I was just eating without restriction. She told me that I had to learn to treat myself with love, the way I treated everyone else in my life. She also became a great friend to me, and I know that she believed that I could get better. Unlike therapists in the past who wanted to "manage my obsession," she believed I could break free and change. Although I did not radically change my habits at that time (what I ate, how often I weighed myself, how often I exercised), Kristy taught me how to begin to have moments of self love.

When I reflect on medical school, I see many missed opportunities for physicians to help me. I saw several specialists at the Mayo Clinic during that time. I would mention my eating disorder history, but once they saw that my body mass index was in the "normal range," they would determine I was fine. No one asked me questions. If I told the doctors that I was eating healthfully and working out, they just moved on to the next question. They didn't ask me what I was eating or how much I was exercising.

Low Points at Low Weights

They didn't know that I was obsessively weighing myself every day. These were amazing doctors at the highest rated hospital in the world, and they knew nothing about eating disorders. Because of this, I truly believed I had to be emaciated in order to qualify as having an active eating disorder. I was still in denial.

— 5 —

Recovery

AFTER MEDICAL SCHOOL, I moved to St. Louis for my pediatric residency, and I finally got to live with my husband. With the stressors of medical school and a long distance relationship behind me, I thought that I would finally care less about being thin. It was much harder to diet with Drew around. He ate real meals and wanted me to eat with him. He asked me if I was alright when I wasn't eating enough or when I went to the bathroom for long periods after big meals. He told me that he thought weighing myself was a bad idea way before any specialist told me to stop weighing myself.

At first, I became more secretive. I could no longer do my weekend binges and my week long fasting. I had to diet when he wasn't around, which meant during the work day or during night shifts when he wasn't with me. I hid my scales in the cupboard beneath the bathroom sink, behind rows of toilet bowl cleaner and extra soap bars. When he found a scale, I would tell him that I wanted to weigh myself "one last time" and then relinquish the scale to him. I had bought and thrown away so many scales in times of exasperation that I would tell him to hide the scale rather than throwing it away. "So I don't ever have to buy one when I need one," I would say.

He would hide it somewhere else in the basement. I once found it in a bedroom drawer beneath stacks of folded sweaters, another time under his bedside reading table. He didn't use it, so

Recovery

he wasn't constantly checking to see if it was in his place. It felt like I was lying to him when I found it and started using it again, pulling it out from my hiding spot as I got ready for work in the mornings. There were a couple times when he walked into the bathroom while I was weighing myself. I would quickly throw a towel or my pajamas over the scale to hide it. He inevitably found out that I'd been weighing myself again when I gained instead of lost weight and became hysterical.

The moment I realized that my problem was not only still present but also too big for me to handle on my own occurred half way through my first year of residency. After several days of team building and celebrating with my co-residents on the annual "intern retreat," which featured all of the junk food you can imagine, I made myself throw up for the first time in months. Drew found out quickly; I had to tell him because he knew something was wrong. Once again, he looked at me not with anger but with sadness. He wanted me to take care of myself, to love myself the way he loved me. Desperate and defeated, I spent the entire day in tears. I stepped on the scale to find out that I had gained three pounds since the start of residency. I was putting my body through the ringer with constant dieting in the midst of a crazy schedule (often eighty hour work weeks), and I was also putting my husband through the ringer. On this day, I decided I didn't need a therapist to help me stop eating and be my ideal body weight; I needed a therapist to help me *recover from an eating disorder* that was preventing me from living a full and meaningful life. It was serious. For the first time in my life, I believed that recovering from my eating disorder was more important than staying skinny. I also realized that if I didn't recover, it would not only affect me, but also Drew.

I chose to go to the office where Gina and Maiya worked because it was only a few miles from where I lived, and I'd read online that some of the therapists specialized in eating disorders. Gina was a therapist, and Maiya was a dietitian, but they often worked together and saw the same patients. There was a key difference between them and my previous therapists, which I noted at my first visit. Even though I had a normal BMI, they believed that I had a severe and dangerous eating disorder requiring immediate and frequent interventions. They did not consider my eating disorder to be less serious just because I was not a "normal" weight. The degree to which I was consumed by thoughts about my weight was enough.

Initially I worked with Maiya, my dietitian, to discuss my eating habits. She taught me that binge eating was always my body's response to restrictive eating (eating less than what my body needed). She labeled so much of what I thought was "normal" or even "healthy" eating as *restrictive*. I learned that it was the most harmful thing I could do to my body for several reasons. Restriction puts your brain and body into states of deprivation. The body and brain truly believe that food is scarce and that they must protect you from starvation (this is an evolutionary response that kept many of our ancestors alive). The longer it is in this state, the more the brain tries to fight back and preserve itself by craving high calorie foods and triggering the behavior of binge eating whenever one finally eats. The body compensates as well. It alters your metabolism and holds onto high calorie food by slowing down digestion (this can cause bloating, constipation, and gastroparesis as well as rapid weight gain). The longer and more often a person restricts, the more the brain and body fight back by binge eating and slowing down metabolism. This sets a person up for even more issues with body image and often triggers even more restriction. It is an endless cycle.

Maiya had me write down everything I ate. I learned that I had been restricting my food intake for so long that my brain believed it had to binge in order to keep me alive. I also realized that I had no idea what "normal eating" looked like. Maiya gave me her guidelines for eating, which she calls "the peaceful plate." A peaceful place includes a serving of fruits or vegetables, a serving of grains or simple carbohydrates, a serving of protein, and a serving of fat. I needed to have all of these different nutrients at each meal in order to keep my body from feeling deprived. I also needed to eat frequently enough, every three to four hours, with snacks of one or two food groups in between meals. I was very afraid at first. I was afraid that I would quickly gain weight with this approach, that I would be triggered to binge eat when I finally allowed myself the foods that I had avoided for a long time. Maiya asked for me to trust her.

Maiya emphasized the importance of balance, not just in nutrition but also in fluid intake, sleep, and exercise. Too much or too little of any of these four things would be noticed by my body, and then would impact my mental, emotional, and spiritual health. My best self needed all of these things working in harmony. She taught me that becoming balanced in physical wellness would allow me to be whole and would then impact the other aspects of my life. "Becoming whole," she would say, "will allow you to be whol-ly you."

This time around in therapy, I had to change my habits and break the cycle of dieting, which was one of the hardest things I've ever had to do. Initially, when I was told I was going to binge eat until I completely stopped restricting my food intake, I was terrified, and I didn't fully commit. I did not trust myself to eat whatever I wanted; it was out of the question. After years of ignoring the cues of hunger and fullness, I didn't remember what they felt like. When I felt well fed, I was afraid; did this mean I had eaten too much? The voice of my eating disorder whispered to me, "If you feel upset about what you ate, then there must be a good reason." In these moments, fear overwhelmed me. I had no way to measure myself, no way to know if my body was spiraling out of control, no way to know if I was gaining pounds that would be twice as hard to lose as they were to gain. On the days when I felt insecure about my appearance, I felt trapped, as if I was not allowed to "fix myself" by dieting.

Through all of it, Drew loved me and encouraged me. He praised me for following the advice of Gina and Maiya. He reassured me when I had moments of panic and wanted me to gain whatever weight might come with the process of recovery. He made it clear that he found my body beautiful and desirable, even if it was changing. On the days that felt the hardest, when I wanted to give up on recovery, he came with me to my appointments with Maiya.

Skinny or Not, Here I Come

Maiya was also very spiritual. During one of our first visits, I told Maiya that I felt like my eating disorder was getting in the way of my relationship with God, and that I also felt like I needed God's help to overcome it. From that point on, Maiya and I talked about my faith at every visit. I began to realize that my eating disorder had served to fill an empty space within me, a space that could only be filled with a relationship with God.

> When I am truly focused on Christ, my body is a temple. When I am truly focused on Christ, my body is not a measure of my goodness of my adequacy. When I am truly focused on Christ, I am but a conduit through which he can enter the world. The eating disorder does not come from a place of Christ, of goodness or love. It does not want to protect me. It wants to scare me. It wants to punish me. It seeks revenge and punishment. If I choose to be a Christian, a follower of Christ, then I cannot also choose the eating disorder. If I choose Christ, I cannot worship a number on a scale or the brief "high" I get from losing weight. If I choose Christ, I cannot prioritize my physical appearance. If I choose Christ, I cannot choose to deceive and manipulate my body. I cannot choose to starve myself.

When I became frustrated or angry with myself, Maiya reminded me of God's love for me. Maiya also knew how much I believed my career was a calling for me. She often asked me what advice I would give a patient regarding my behaviors. She helped me to realize that the way I treated myself was so different from the way I treated others, and the way I loved other people, including my patients, was how I should be loving myself. She also reminded me that my eating disorder kept me from being the best doctor I could be, the best version of myself. It held me back from what mattered to me.

It became apparent to me during recovery that I had numerous double standards. I held myself to different standards than others. Not only have I never considered treating another person as awfully as I have treated myself; I also have never expected perfection from others the way I demand it from myself. Maiya's probing questions made me think about this. If I believed that I should achieve things no one else could, then did that mean I believed that I was better than other people? Was there a piece of me that was actually vain? Was my vanity holding onto my eating disorder? I wrote about it.

> I do not feel more drawn to or more enamored by people who are thin. I do not believe people who are thin or physically beautiful are better or more deserving of love. I do not believe people deserve praise for their physical appearance. I do not believe someone has to be thin in order to deserve dessert or a day of laziness on the couch or a bra that fits rather than suppressing their supple breasts. I do not believe a person should ever go to bed with their stomach growling. I do not believe a person should reject all joy and happiness until they reach their ideal weight. I do not believe a person needs to have a perfect body or relationship with their body in order to be a good mother. And yet, I treat myself as if I believe all of these things. Why should I hold myself to a different standard than others? I once thought it was because I felt inferior to others and needed to prove myself, but when I reflect on all the different rules that I apply to myself, I realize that it may be just the opposite. Why do I have to be perfect? Why do I have to attain unreachable standards? Do I believe I'm superhuman? Do I believe I'm different than everyone else? Does this eating disorder always feel so selfish to me because it comes from a place of me wanting to be better than everyone else? Why is this the measure of my success?

I often shared my written reflections with Maiya because she also loved to write. She praised me for my writing and celebrated it as an important part of my recovery. When I told her that I had decided to write about my journey in order to help others, she encouraged me to do this. When I had times that were difficult, she asked me if I'd been writing or taking time to focus on my spirituality. She helped me to realize that I could not be my best and most stable self without taking time to nurture my faith and to write. These things, I realized, were often one in the same for me.

Meanwhile, Gina slowly unpacked the history of my eating disorder. As the memories came back to me, some of them after years of suppression, I shared them with Gina. She often identified factors that contributed to the eating disorder's development. I was a perfectionist. I was made fun of by my peers and felt like I wasn't accepted for being me. My mother had also struggled with an eating disorder, I realized, which is why she had demonstrated such unhealthy eating behaviors.

Gina believed that my mom's eating habits and values had a big influence on me as a child and continued to impact me as an adult. She encouraged me to talk to my mom about my eating disorder, my recovery, and my triggers. Mama had always supported me when I had ups and downs (in my feelings and my weight), but she had also assumed that I needed to be thin in order to be happy. I have always known that she wanted the best for me in life and would support me no matter what, but I was afraid that I would hurt her by asking her to support my decision to recover no matter what that meant about my weight. I was also afraid I would hurt her by asking her not to discuss her diets or her weight with me. I was wrong, though. Mama responded with grace and understanding, and she told me how proud she was that I was getting the help I needed. She asked me many questions about my therapy and encouraged me to stick with it. She apologized for influencing my eating disorder, which I knew was never her intention. After talking more with Mama about her experiences, I realize that her beliefs about weight were passed down to her from her mother and from the southern culture. Our discussions were healing for me, and she became my biggest encouragement as I attempted to write this book. Every time I told her about one of my struggles, she reminded me, "you should write about it."

Gina also helped me to move past the state of denial I'd been living in for so many years. I have an eating disorder. I will not ever be one of those "normal people" who can just go on a diet, lose a few pounds, and stop being on a diet. My diets have always dictated my life, taken me to a place of self hatred, reignited the flame of my eating disorder. Like a recovered alcoholic, I have to protect myself from triggers (such as dieting). I told Gina about all of the odd ways in which I'd restricted my food intake. I told her about the times I chewed up sweets and spit them out, the habit I'd developed of drinking fluids constantly to keep myself from feeling hungry, the way I'd take tiny bites and push my food around my plate to feel full sooner, the amount of diet soda I drank instead of snacking, and how I'd sometimes sucked on sweet tarts at bedtime to help with hunger pains as I drifted off to sleep. I expected to see a look of disgust or surprise on her face, but she always nodded, smiled the slightest bit, and said, "I've heard this before, and it's very common in people with eating disorders." Not only did I feel understood; I also recognized that I have a real eating disorder, and I deserve for it to be taken seriously.

Gina often emphasized that recovery was not linear. It had ups and downs, but the trajectory was up-going. When I "fell down" or started to slide back into my eating disorder habits, she helped me to focus on how I'd gotten back up. Every time I had a hiccup in my recovery, she reminded me of the last hiccup. Every time, my response to the problem and my ability to quickly get back on track was quicker and better than before. Gina helped me to see the bigger picture.

Gina also helped me to become painfully aware of my values. Like Kristy, she wanted me to make a list of who I was and who I wanted to be. This was helpful. However, she took it a step farther. As we discussed my fears of weight gain and the self hatred I felt when I was not as thin as I wanted to be, I realized that I was incredibly invested in my appearance. I realized that my values were consistent with my Christian faith, but my obsessions with my weight and appearance were not. A big part of me was superficial, judgmental, and obsessed with the material world. I recognized that I often looked at other people and made judgments about them based on their weight or how they dressed. I had fat bias, not just towards myself but towards others. I assumed that people who were larger than me were unhappy about it, and I assumed that people who were thinner than me were happy about it. I also assumed everyone who was thin was dieting. I associated thin-ness with success; if they looked good, they must have earned it. Gina helped me to correct my beliefs about this. She reminded me of the variability in human metabolism, something that I am surprised I did not consider sooner.

It was difficult to be honest with myself about these things, to admit to myself that some of my values needed to change. Gina recommended focusing on my other values instead, developing the other things in my life that were important to me, such as my friendships and my faith. She also prompted me to ask several of my closest friends to tell me why they loved me. None of the reasons had anything to do with my weight or my appearance. They were about my ability to love, to be kind, to make people laugh, to build others up, to share joy and optimism. I wrote the reasons down in my journal. I looked at them whenever things got hard again, if ever I began to doubt who I was without my weight.

I asked Gina to help me get past the value I didn't want. She encouraged me to spend less time focusing on it, to look in the mirror sparingly (only when doing my hair and makeup), to get rid of my full length mirror, to throw away any clothes that didn't fit, to take less pictures of myself, and to get off Instagram (or at least stop following anything that felt superficial). She told me to ask my close friends not to talk about weight or diets, to stop watching reality television shows glorifying superficial people, to destroy my scale and never have one around, and to stop going to the gym in favor of taking walks outside or doing yoga instead. Focusing on the superficial would only tempt me to care more about my appearance and my weight, and it would never be worth it.

Gina also taught me how to re-frame my thoughts, to recognize the triggers for the eating disorder mentality and my automatic thoughts in response. The automatic thoughts were often lies that my eating disorder created, and I needed to correct them before they led to overwhelming emotions which were hard to fight off. I learned that I had to prevent myself from ending up in a hyper emotional state, because once in that state, logic was not very helpful. Such a state was often caused by me weighing myself, seeing an unflattering picture of myself, or relapsing (i.e.

binge eating and purging). I learned that the best way for me to get out of such an emotional place was to express my feelings (crying, etc.) and then do something to ground myself (deep breathing, a shower, a leisurely walk outside). I often found that I could disconnect from an overwhelming feeling when I did these things. Often, after the activity, the feelings didn't seem as powerful. The most helpful solution was doing a guided Christian meditation while deep breathing. It sometimes allowed me to drift to sleep, and I always woke up feeling calm and more logical.

I started seeing Gina and Maiya in December of my intern year of residency, and it wasn't until two years later that I reached a place that consistently felt like "recovery". It would be dishonest not to mention the many relapses I endured over a two year period. It was difficult to break the habits of a lifetime, difficult to learn to ignore the loud voice of the eating disorder and begin to notice the long-ignored voices of my body's needs. Apart from therapy, my writing was key. Once I began writing, I also began sharing with others. It was as if writing had given me the courage to talk about it openly.

With each friend I told, I felt more empowered. I realized that I was the only person who had ever defined me by my weight. All of my friends and family supported my goal of recovery. This helped because so much of my fear of recovery and weight gain was about what other people would think of me. Every time I shared, I would realize that people were relieved I was loving myself, and that they'd been loving me all along *in spite of* my thin-ness, not because of it.

— 6 —

Relapses

WHEN I BEGAN MY therapy with Gina and Maiya, I changed my actions. I got rid of some of my pathological behaviors. I stopped starving myself, I stopped purging when I binged or "ate past fullness." I started allowing myself "breaks" from exercise, skipping the gym when I was physically exhausted from work. I stopped weighing myself every day. I wrote down everything I ate in my food diary. Still, I continued to have anxiety and even episodes of panic when I felt like I was losing the control I'd harnessed for so long. I trusted neither my body nor myself, so while I did avoid using a scale every day, I was constantly looking for other ways to measure myself. For a long time, even though I knew I was "eating like a normal person," every time I undressed myself I was disgusted and terrified.

During those times, when prompted by Gina or Maiya, I could easily list many ways in which my life was *better* than before. I had more energy and stamina, fewer headaches, better ability to concentrate at work, less anxiety at meal times, and less binge eating. Despite all of these positives, I still had moments of complete devastation. At the time, I felt like I was choosing between having a healthy and well-fed body and having a thin and beautiful body that I felt comfortable in. Much of the "overwhelm" came from the fear that I would keep gaining and gaining weight. I felt like I was a top spinning out of control and would never stop spinning.

Relapses

I feared how much more I would hate my body when it got even larger. Maiya kept telling me that if I kept feeding my body and didn't give into restriction, then my body would eventually reach its "set point". I worried that my set point might be much larger than the body I'd forced myself to have for so many years. All of these thoughts and feelings would sometimes trigger me to either restrict or overeat. The more afraid I felt of my body, the less ability I had to listen to what it wanted and give it what it needed.

Some of my setbacks happened in response to weight gain, even if it was a negligible amount. If I perceived a change in my weight, despite knowing it was part of my recovery, I panicked. The anxiety I felt in the setting of weight gain was so powerful that I addressed it the only way I knew how: I tried to lose weight again. I would slowly stop writing down my meals and then skipping snacks, and then I would skip meals and make excuses. I would buy another scale and hide it somewhere I thought Drew wouldn't find it. I would convince myself that I was doing something that everyone had to do from time to time. I would weigh myself every day, allow my mood to soar or come crashing down in response to the number, and eat as little as possible to function. Each time, I would end up binge eating, hating myself even more than before, and feeling trapped and depressed. Whenever I ended up in the depressed state again, I would eventually decide I needed to go back to therapy, because following the instructions of my eating disorder made things worse. Most of the time, the process of writing allowed me to remember who I was apart from the eating disorder and why I wanted to change.

> It never happens like I envision it will. It never happens like the voice says it will. This time, I will be "a normal person." I will lose 5 pounds and feel better. I will put the scale away and maintain all of the weight loss. This time, if the weight doesn't do what I think it will, I will remain level headed and go on with my life. This time, I won't allow my entire day to be consumed with thoughts about how much happier I would be if I could be skinny again. This time, my day won't be filled with thoughts about food. I won't fixate or obsess. Once again, you are the

Skinny or Not, Here I Come

thief that comes to steal and slaughter and destroy. Once again, you are the antithesis of that which gives abundant life. Why have I found myself in this trap again? My eating disorder is not killing me. It is not keeping me in a hospital for tube feeds and electrolyte abnormalities. It has not caused me to fall out of (or grow out of) the normal BMI range or develop issues with my bone health or cardiac health. No, my eating disorder is more insidious. It is a thief and a demon rather than a killer. It lingers in the depths of my thoughts and my emotions, and it preys upon my joy. Why must I measure my body? Why must I look at every picture taken of myself and compare my body to the way it looked at its skinniest? Why can't I trust that I am enough without the status of being thin?

My biggest relapse occurred one year into my treatment with Gina and Maiya. I purchased yet another scale, started weighing myself daily, and started restricting after the holidays. This diet felt more difficult than previous diets, not because I was restricting to a more severe degree, but because I felt miserable. Physically, it was more difficult than previous diets because my body gave me hunger cues consistently, and I noticed changes in my energy level without consistent meals. Emotionally, not only did I feel frustration with myself and some degree of self hatred (feelings I had always felt while dieting), but I also felt guilty. I had to hide the scale from Drew and respond "yes" to him when he asked me if I'd eaten my meals and snacks that day. I was lying not only to him, but also to myself. I was sacrificing so much of myself to honor a superficial cultural standard. I was disgusted with myself, but I did not feel like I had a choice.

Inevitably, that diet led me to drink too much at holiday parties, binge eat every time I finally allowed myself to eat, and hate myself even more (the only times I've ever had too much to drink was when I was filled up on alcohol instead of food). Around this time, I had a memorable conversation with my little sister, Flynn. While on a walk outside, I told her that I was struggling with feelings about my weight yet again. I asked her for advice, admitting that I was envious of her for not obsessing over her weight. She

Relapses

confessed that she hadn't always felt good about herself. She said that her weight had fluctuated a lot while she was in college because she dieted on and off, and she had felt very insecure when she gained weight. Whenever she came home from college, our mom would tell her she "looked amazing" if she'd lost weight, and say nothing about her appearance if she'd gained weight. She felt like Mama was prouder of her weight than her accomplishments in school. Somehow, Flynn eventually decided that it wasn't worth it to constantly fight her body's natural size; it didn't make her happy. She had a successful career, tons of friends, and a serious boyfriend who loved her. She didn't need to be skinnier to love herself. She wanted to take care of her body, not punish it. After hearing all of this, I came to respect and admire her in a whole new way. Despite being raised under the same influences as me, Flynn had chosen not to let those influences dictate her body image or her happiness.

My turning point happened the next week. I was rotating in the pediatric intensive care unit, working twelve to fourteen hour days every day of the week (with the occasional twenty-eight hour shift) in a physically, intellectually, and emotionally demanding environment. I could not function, could not be the doctor I need to be, without eating well. As I stood in the ICU during one of the longest mornings I had ever had, feeling self-conscious about my body but also hungry and tired, I thought to myself, "It would be so much easier for me to stick to my diet and be skinny if I had a different job." It was the first time in my life I had ever, even for a flicker, questioned my career choice. Even though it was a fleeting thought, I'd valued being thin above my vocation. This was not okay with me; this was not who I wanted to be.

I went back to therapy just a week or so later. This time, I took Drew with me. He sat next to me throughout my appointment with Maiya, holding my hand and encouraging me as I cried. I told Maiya I wanted to start over from scratch at that appointment. I wanted to be more honest with myself and with Maiya about little "slip ups" in my plan: the times I skipped snacks when I was hungry, the times I used laxatives, the times I avoided certain foods that I deemed "bad." Drew promised to hold me accountable. He forgave me time and time again for temporarily abandoning my recovery. He never stopped looking at me with love and compassion. I do not know how I would have recovered without him.

The next setback in my recovery occurred after I had begun writing this book, during my time working from home due to the COVD-19 pandemic. I had more free time than I'd had in years, so I began taking time each day to write. I began adding my faith back into my life on a daily basis, even if it was just to read the daily mass scripture or do a twenty-minute Christian meditation on my phone. I began to connect with aspects of myself that I had left behind in the midst of being a busy resident. I began to read novels, take long bubble baths, and sit outside just to enjoy nature. I would look at myself in the mirror infrequently during this time, but when I did, I would think to myself, "I look curvier, and my body is changing, but this is good."

On one of these days, I caught a glimpse of myself in the web-cam while visiting friends and felt something akin to panic. I couldn't decide if I was gaining weight or if I had body dysmorphia. Was it all in my head? I tried on some shorts that had always been tight. I told myself lies as I pulled on the shorts: "This will be helpful. This is for your own good." The shorts didn't zip. I *had* gained weight since the last time I wore these shorts. It wasn't "all in my head". The loud voice of the eating disorder demanded that I buy a scale and start another diet, that I fix myself before it was "too late". Yet this time, there was another voice, fighting back. It was a voice that believed that I had to find a way to be okay with my new weight because it was a healthy weight, a voice that believed my body was better off gaining some weight, a voice that believed I was healing. For the first time in my life, both voices were equally powerful. I felt warfare within myself. At such a turning point, I had two choices. I could give into the voices and lose the weight for the millionth time, or I could finally learn to love myself at a different size. The latter was difficult. In many ways, it was more difficult than giving in.

This time, I didn't buy a scale. This time, I didn't cancel my appointments with Gina or Maiya. This time, I didn't stop writing

Relapses

or praying just because I started weighing myself. This time, my self hatred didn't end because of an episode of bingeing or purging. It ended because I decided to end it. It ended because I decided that I didn't want to be that person any more, the one who checks her weight every morning and determines her level of happiness based on the digits, the one who can't have a normal meal without becoming upset, the one who eventually *does* end up binge eating. I didn't want to be someone who prioritized their weight over their career, relationships, and faith. I didn't want to go back to that dark place that I was in last time I was "skinny enough" for my liking, a place of intermittent panic attacks, headaches, fatigue, and social isolation. I still wanted to be thin, but I kept asking myself, "At what cost?"

> Will I make my body pay again- will I harm my renal function from "skinny teas" and overhydration? Will I hurt my esophagus from purging after my body forces me to eat crazy amounts because it was so deprived? Will I sacrifice my intellect again- studying without fully comprehending what I'm studying because I am starving? Will I sacrifice my relationships again, by skipping social functions because there will be food and drinks there, by hiding bathroom scales from my husband, by becoming introverted and isolated when I am on a diet? Will I sacrifice my happiness again by depriving myself of the joy that comes from food and being well nourished and energized?

This time, I fought back stronger than ever before. I scheduled more appointments with Gina and Maiya. I committed myself to the process of healing again. I focused on my identity. Whenever I began to question myself based on my physical appearance or size, I thought back to the "list" I'd created of who I wanted to be. I replaced the weighing myself with prayers upon waking. I replaced the ample time spent in front of the mirror with longer and more mindful breakfasts. I replaced the thoughts of "am I enough?" with reminders of God's love for me and Drew's love for me. Slowly, I became more free from the mind-consuming trap of the eating disorder.

There were other lessons I still had to learn. Once I stopped replacing all of my problems with eating disorder thoughts, I had to learn to experience and work through negative emotions that *weren't* about body image. I have heard addicts talk about the need to learn how to cope with and experience life without drugs or alcohol. I have had to do the same without my eating disorder. As the COVID-19 pandemic dragged on, some of my work was online rather than in the hospital, so my life was less busy. Drew went back to work while I worked from home, so I had ample time alone in silence. I felt my identity slipping away without my normal interactions with patients. I started to focus on my body again. I had not been restricting, binge eating, or weighing myself. I was wearing gym clothes every day, and I didn't have the trigger of being disappointed when seeing pictures of myself (no pictures were taken during those days). What, then, was wrong with me?

It was then that I realized that I was attempting to find my self-worth in being thin. Despite being a Christian with self proclaimed values that were *not* about the superficial, I deeply valued being thin, and I longed for the success I felt from weight loss. The value of thin-ness had become so essential to who I was; without it, I struggled to know where to focus my energy. I mentioned this in my therapy sessions, and Maiya and Gina urged me to make a list of the things that defined me *besides my body*. I posted the list on my laptop and mirror: "a conduit for Christ to enter the world, Drew's wife, a doctor to sick children, a future mother, a published author, a great friend, and still becoming what God wants me to be".

I learned that any negative emotion, no matter how unrelated, could trigger me to focus on my weight. Drew's dental practice endured a lot of changes during the pandemic. Rather than just doing clinical work as a dentist, he began doing lots of work to help the business run well. I wasn't used to his job being busier than mine. As I thought about this one evening when he stayed late at work, as I rode the stationary bike, I suddenly became extremely angry at myself. I decided that I should ride the bike longer, faster, harder. I began to work out aggressively, telling myself that I "needed it,"

Relapses

that I was getting fat. The self hatred that I was all too familiar with began to show its face.

I caught myself. I got off the bike. I recognized that I had bad feelings, but they weren't about my weight. I was disappointed that Drew's job was requiring more of him, that I was getting less time with him. My disappointment had quickly morphed into self blame. "Maybe there's a reason he's not home yet. Maybe I'm the reason. Maybe I'm not a good enough wife. Maybe I'm not desirable enough." I didn't know how to feel lonely or angry. So I'd quickly, easily, seamlessly tapped into the emotions that my eating disorder once taught me. I'd shifted into a headspace and an emotional point of view that felt normal for me. The emotions of self hatred and self discipline and self-directed anger flooded in. The desire to drive myself into the ground with a painful workout, weigh myself, start another diet, and scratch the word "FAT" into my arm returned. For the first time in my life I realized that I was *choosing* to feel these things. I was choosing to fall back into the painful mentality of my eating disorder, to hide in self destruction, because I was too afraid of feeling anything else. I was too afraid of feeling lonely, too afraid of feeling jealous of the time my husband was spending with his job, too afraid of feeling unfamiliar sources of pain. By choosing to take my feelings out on myself and my body, I was making things worse for myself.

I had to learn—and am still learning—to sit with and acknowledge my feelings, no matter what they are. There have been other challenges during my recovery apart from processing feelings. There have been "triggers" that pulled me back into my eating disorder thoughts and feelings. I am still hyper aware of other people's comments about dieting and weight. I am uncomfortable with the terms "fat" and "obese." Despite being a physician, I even struggle with the term "overweight."

I was recently sitting on a boat in a lake, surrounded by friends. Lying in the sun in our swimsuits, as I relished in the new feeling of being somewhat comfortable in my body, a little boy rode by on a jet ski. He was plump, wearing a swim top and a life jacket, with rosy cheeks, fair freckled skin, and gorgeous

Skinny or Not, Here I Come

red hair. He was smiling and happy, enjoying the lake. Someone began to giggle.

"Look at that fat redhead," one person said. Everyone else chimed in with their laughter. I felt uncomfortable with this and sad for the boy. I said that he looked like he was having fun and that I liked his red hair, hoping to change the course of conversation.

"Oh, look, he has fat parents, too," another person said. Two bigger-bodied adults with life jackets drove confidently by as the people on the boat giggled. I squirmed in my seat, hoping the discussion had ended.

The first person who'd spoken chimed in, "Can you believe these people? They have no respect for themselves!"

I spoke up, "I feel sad for them, because it must be so hard to be overweight in our society. I'm sure they don't want to be fat and are trying not to be. I'm actually happy for them and impressed that they are able to enjoy themselves on the lake in spite of it."

He responded, "They don't need us to feel sad for them. That's part of the problem. So many people in our country refuse to take personal responsibility for their own health and become a drain on our health care system."

I said, "I don't think it's that simple. As someone who is *still* in therapy for an eating disorder, I have had many times when I have not been able to control what I was eating, no matter how hard I tried. I'm sure that people who are very overweight struggle with similar problems, and it's not their fault."

"I don't think it's the same thing at all. It *is* their fault. They need to take initiative and do something about it. This seems to be a bigger problem in America than anywhere else. You don't see people in Europe like this," he replied, his voice getting louder.

I felt unheard, even a little attacked. In trying to stand up for these strangers and interrupt the fat shaming, my ideas had become a target. I couldn't continue to partake in the one-sided conversation, so I moved to the other side of the boat, crying silently behind my hat and sunglasses.

At the end of the weekend, a picture had been posted on Instagram of all of the girls on the boat. I assessed myself in the

Relapses

picture on my way home from the lake. I wish I could tell you that I'd evolved so much that I simply deleted the picture from my phone and moved on with my day. Instead, my eyes expertly scanned the photo, critiquing every contour of my body, honing in on my stomach. I felt the self hatred build up inside of me. For the rest of the day, it felt worse than ever before. I'd had a reprieve from the feeling for months, and it hurt more because it was no longer familiar. I also knew that I could not let myself surrender. I knew that the easy way out (buying a scale, losing some weight again, conforming to society's standards instead of fighting against society) was wrong for me. I could not back down again. Instead, with Drew's encouragement, I cried, listened to a guided meditation prayer, and began to write again.

I know that I can choose to go along with a culture I don't believe in and allow it to change me in the process, or I can choose to stand up and fight for what matters to me. I suppose all the important battles in life are like this. The fight may not always be easy, but it's the right thing to do. Over time, I bet it won't be as painful.

This experience is one example of how challenging it can be to hold strong to the changes I have made when I am influenced by others. I am still susceptible to the old thoughts and feelings that flood in when other people influence me. It takes courage for me to speak up when conversations about weight ensue. I feel strong enough to do it with family and close friends, but I am still afraid to do it in every setting. From the nurses at work who discuss the weight they need to lose, to the very lean and athletic friend who told me she was "avoiding carbs" as we sat together in our swimsuits, I am learning how to respond. I am learning how to stand up for myself and the countless others this problem affects.

To be honest, part of my publishing this book is just that. It's a sort of "coming out of the closet" for all of the world to see. It's an admission of my sins and struggles and a plea for accountability. The thing is, I am not sure that I am strong enough to stick to all of the changes I have made if I ignore everything going on around me. I am not satisfied to stop there. If there is a chance for me to help others reach a place closer to self love and acceptance, to realize their lifelong struggles with their bodies don't have to be forever, I have to try. For a long time, I believed that I would eventually reach a point in my recovery at which I felt "finished" recovering. While it is true that the temptations and challenges I have surrounding body image arise much less often than they once did, they are not gone. Perhaps one day they will subside completely, but right now, though they exist, they are quiet voices with very little power over me.

One of the reasons I am able to turn away from the voices is because I no longer trust them. They were never helpful to me. I remind myself that even when my eating disorder sought to create body satisfaction, it inevitably led to body hatred, which led to me to punish myself. It was draining. It sucked the life out of me, causing me to self-isolate, to be less upbeat, less forgiving, less imaginative, less productive in my work, and less capable of loving others. I remind myself that the quest to weigh less is not worth *being* less. When the struggle over weight or not eating becomes a distraction from life goals, it *becomes* a life goal. I remind myself that I am not willing to waste more of my life on such a goal.

I have learned from Gina and Maiya that recovery is not linear. It has many curves, but each downturn is followed by an upturn bigger than the upturn before. Over time, the trajectory is still up. When I have a day that feels like I'm taking a downward turn on the recovery curve—maybe I "felt fat", skipped a meal, exercised or ate compulsively, or cried about how I looked in a picture—I acknowledge it. I identify that I have taken a step back, then I take a minute to notice all of the thoughts my mind is generating on autopilot. Many of the thoughts trigger fear: "I'm losing my progress," "I messed up my body irreversibly," "I look different and people will notice," or "I fell off the wagon and it will be so hard to get back on."

These thoughts, I recognize, are hyperbolic. I can let them control my feelings and then impact my actions, or I can *choose* to re-frame the events in a realistic light. "I had a moment where old habits crept back in. That's normal. That's okay. I'm still in control, and I'm still in recovery. My body can handle this; my metabolism

Relapses

is competent. I will get back on my eating schedule and be more in tune to listening to and following my body's cues. I will be more patient with myself and my body. I have done nothing wrong." The anxiety begins to subside. I am able to remember who I am apart from my body image and even my body itself. No matter how skinny or fat I feel (although I now know that these are *not* feelings), I am alive in this world right now, and my body is what allows me to be on this earth. I want to use all of my passion and energy for something more meaningful than dieting.

At each hiccup, I find myself able to recover and move forward more quickly than the last time. I will not pretend that I'm not disappointed when setbacks happen. However, I no longer wallow in self-hatred when they do. I remind myself of all the tools that I've developed, and I apply them. I am better at using these tools each time. I am stronger and more capable of self love than I once was. Only I can be the one to turn away from the eating disorder path and choose the path that is best for me, the path of self love and forgiveness, of goodness and God. I will keep choosing this path, no matter how many times I have to choose it.

— 7 —

Eating Disorders, God, and Addiction

THE FIRST TIME I doubted the existence of God, I was five years old. I attended a Presbyterian kindergarten, and there was a daily time for Bible verses and discussion. On the day we discussed the concept of hell, I came home from school and cried. "Mama, I don't think I believe in God," I frantically explained. She told me that if I was that upset about not believing in God, then I must believe in God at least a little.

I have always longed to feel connected to God, and like everyone else, I have had ups and downs in my spiritual life. I often feel most connected to God when I have meaningful experiences with my patients, when I sit in mass with my husband, and when I get to share with others how my faith changed as a result of my experience as a cancer patient.

When I begin to drift away from God, I don't always notice immediately. When I am busy, when my mind is actively engaged, when I feel I have a strong purpose in my everyday life, or when I am with family, I feel fine. On the other hand, when I have the time, or take the time, to sit alone in silence and think, I often come back to a place of yearning, unrest, and anxiety. There is always something missing without God. So many times, when something felt "missing," I assumed I needed to better myself by losing weight. I am not sure that my eating disorder developed in childhood because of a need for God that wasn't being met, but I fell back on it time and time again as an adult. In times of anxiety, restlessness, or general dissatisfaction with life, whenever something was missing in my identity or my sense of peace, I weighed myself and started dieting again. It was as if I needed to fill the hole in my heart with something, and I kept choosing the wrong thing. I kept choosing sin instead of God.

A Benedictine monk once told me that he defined sin as "that which separates us from God." If this is what sin is, then my eating disorder has been the greatest source of sin in my life thus far. Somehow, that hasn't made it easier for me to reject it. I have come to believe that an eating disorder is more complicated than many sins because it is also a mental illness. It is not something anyone asks for or decides to pursue. It is created from the perfect storm of genetics, personality traits, and environmental factors (family and culture). This is the case for most mental illnesses, especially addictions.

However, perhaps unlike other mental illnesses and addictions, the eating disorder is uniquely tied to specific sins. By its very nature, an obsession with one's physical appearance is both vain and selfish. An eating disorder may often be an attempt to have control or power, but (as in my case) it is often tied to a desire to be very thin. If my culture and my upbringing had not taught me that thin was beautiful and preferred, I might not have developed anorexia, but I would have undoubtedly fallen into the grips of another sin. The eating disorder is also tied to self hatred and a desire to punish the self, which I firmly believe is also a sin (or in some cases, an inappropriate interpretation of religious teachings).

While I believe that an eating disorder is never initially a *choice,* I do think in my case, after cognitive behavioral therapy and re nourishment, it became a choice. It was a choice to prioritize my weight over my health and my life. It was a choice to choose the scale and quit therapy whenever life felt difficult, time and time again. Like other sins, my choice—my eating disorder—pulled me into a place of self-isolation, self-hatred, and self-absorption.

When Lacey told me to "give it all to God," I had never before considered asking God to help me recover from my eating disorder. Recovery from the eating disorder seemed counteractive to the goals of my Catholic faith. Wasn't I supposed to deny my physical self, to fast in order to become closer to God? Weren't sloth and gluttony the deadly sins? I misconstrued my friend's advice and asked God to help me eat less and lose weight. At that point, I truly believed my desire for food was the main problem. During my weekly Eucharist, my mind was filled with confessions about overeating and prayers begging God for control over my flawed willpower. I truly believed that if I stopped binge eating and controlled my addiction to food, if I reached my goal weight where I could be happy with myself, then I would have no issues and could actually focus on my relationship with God. I see now that my addiction was never to food; it was to dieting. My sin was never overeating; it was under eating so much that my brain triggered me to overeat to help me survive.

My prayers were focused on myself, not the people I loved. I thanked God when I stepped on the scale and saw a number that was lower than the day before, or even the same as the day before if I had recently binged. I wasn't thanking God for my health, my loved ones, or my career. I wasn't asking God to help me learn to love myself. I was asking God to help me become more worthy of his love and my self love by denying myself. After I started seeing Maiya, I realized that I needed God to help me in other ways. I needed God to help me let go of the values and beliefs that landed on me in childhood. I needed God to help free me from my internal struggle. I needed God to be a model of radical self love for me, the type of self love that I had never experienced before.

I came to believe that God was never "above" helping me with my eating disorder. Humans, as living beings created in God's image, depend on the nourishment of food for survival. According to biology and evolution, food is meant to be enjoyed and sought after. God did not intend for any living creatures to starve or punish themselves. God made the body to function as an intuitive machine in regards to food, and my eating disorder got in the way of that. When I accepted these things, I began to notice all of the ways in which my eating disorder had served as a wedge between me and God and as a replacement for God. My desire to find fulfillment in being thin was above my desire to be close to God. There was a time when I would have chosen thin-ness over anything else.

I began to read and listen to Christian scripture with more open mindedness, trying to apply it to my struggles. It became apparent to me that the topics of food and physical body are not only mentioned literally quite frequently; they are also used as important metaphors in both the old and new testaments. In the creation story, when God creates the world, he says, "Behold, I have given you every plant yielding seed that is on the surface of all the earth, and every tree which has fruit yielding seed; it shall be food for you."[1] Later, God addresses the first humans, "Every moving thing that is alive shall be food for you; I give all to you, as I gave the green plant."[2]

In the book of Psalms, God is thought to demonstrate his love for his people with food. The passages "For He has satisfied the thirsty soul, And the hungry He has filled with what is good,"[3] "He causes the grass to grow for the cattle, And vegetation for the labor of man, So that he may bring forth food from the earth, And wine which makes man's heart glad, So that he may make his face glisten with oil, And food that sustains man's heart,"[4] and "He gives food to all flesh, For His lovingkindness is everlasting,"[5] exemplify this use of food.

In the Gospel of John, Jesus states, "I am the bread of life; he who comes to Me will not hunger, and he who believes in Me will never thirst."[6] He is not undermining the need for physical nutrition, but comparing its level of importance to that of spiritual nourishment. Matthew's Gospel includes a similar passage: "Man shall not live on bread alone, but on every word that proceeds out

---

1. Genesis 1:29
2. Genesis 9:3
3. Psalm 107:9
4. Psalm 104:14–15
5. Psalm 136:25
6. John 6:35

of the mouth of God."[7] Even the Beatitudes include the food-based imagery, "Blessed are those who hunger and thirst for righteousness, for they shall be satisfied."[8]

Two of the miracles Jesus performed, including what is believed to have been his first miracle, centered around providing enough sustenance to satisfy large groups of people. In John's Gospel, he tells the story of the wedding at Cana.[9] When the party runs out of wine, Jesus's mother asks him for help. After Jesus tells the servants to fill containers with water and serve some of it to the waiter, the waiter is impressed, referring to it as better than the wine before. John notes that this miracle was the first of Jesus's signs, and that it "manifested his glory, and His disciples believed in Him."[10]

Luke's Gospel tells about the feeding of the five thousand, during which Jesus turned five loaves of bread and two fish into enough food for everyone at the gathering, and "they all ate and were satisfied; and the broken pieces which they had left over were picked up, twelve baskets full."[11]

These miracle stories demonstrate the importance of food and drink to Jesus. It seems that nourishment is not only necessary for humans; it is a way in which Christ expresses love to his people and provides for them. In John's Gospel, he proclaimed at a large gathering of people, "If anyone is thirsty, let him come to Me and drink."[12]

Many scholars have interpreted Jesus' identity as a human being to be indicative of the importance of the human body. Embodiment is central to the Christian faith and message. The human body was created by God and is said to be similar to that of God: "God said, 'Let Us make man in Our image, according to Our likeness.'"[13]

7. Matthew 4:4
8. Matthew 5:6
9. John 2:1–11
10. John 2:11
11. Luke 9:17
12. John 7:37
13. Genesis 1:26

Eating Disorders, God, and Addiction

Both the Old and New Testament include commentary about the physical body. In Paul's letters, he writes, "Whether, then, you eat or drink or whatever you do, do all to the glory of God."[14] Paul also asks the Corinthians, "Or do you not know that your body is a temple of the Holy Spirit who is in you?"[15] He implies that the body is necessary for the Holy Spirit's presence. He then suggests that it is wrong to mistreat the body: "For he who eats and drinks, eats and drinks judgment to himself if he does not judge the body rightly."[16] He seems to be endorsing the practices of honoring the body and listening to its needs.

At the same time, in the Gospel of Matthew, Jesus minimizes the importance of food and the body, saying, "For this reason I say to you, do not be worried about your life, as to what you will eat or what you will drink; nor for your body, as to what you will put on. Is not life more than food, and the body more than clothing?"[17] He suggests that these concerns are not meant to cause us worry or distress. We are meant to trust God about these things rather than obsess over them.

After searching for all the passages in the Bible concerning food and the body, I found many ways in which they were used as metaphors. Somehow, I had sat through mass for years and never even noticed that the whole service revolved around Jesus's message to "take and eat" his body. How could my relationships with food and my body be trivial to God or my faith in light of all of this? Food, it seems, is a vessel through which God shows us love (through the Eucharist) and a reminder of our dependence on God (through our nourishment). I am certain that my fragmented relationships with food and my body were not "normal," "natural," or anything close to what God intended for living beings, especially humans, to experience.

After concluding that the eating disorder is a mix of both mental illness and sin, I began to reflect on stories about Jesus

14. 1 Corinthians 10:31
15. 1 Corinthians 6:19
16. 1 Corinthians 11:29
17. Matthew 6:25

and healing. It occurred to me that sins are sometimes referred to as "cured" in scripture. This suggests that sin is not always something we choose for ourselves; sometimes, it is more like a disease. For example, in the book of James, Jesus says, "confess your sins to one another, and pray for one another so that you may be healed."[18] In the Gospel of Luke, when a man with leprosy says to Jesus, "Lord, if You are willing, You can make me clean,"[19] Jesus responds by touching him and saying, "I am willing; be cleansed."[20] Even though leprosy was a disease associated with great shame and social stigma during that time, Jesus did not blame the man or hesitate to heal the man. Whatever the sin or the illness, Jesus wanted to help.

In Mark's story about a crippled man, forgiveness of sins is interchangeable with physical healing. Jesus asks, "Is it easier for me to tell this crippled man that his sins are forgiven or to tell him to get up and pick up his mat and go home?" The crippled man is then able to walk.[21] Human problems were important to Jesus, who says in the Gospel of Thomas, "If you bring forth that which is within you, it will save you. If you do not bring it forth, it will destroy you."[22] We are meant, it seems, to ask God for the help we need. The lines between illness and sin are often blurred in the gospels. I do not believe nor wish to suggest that physical illnesses are punishments for sin. I do, however, think that these stories illustrate human problems (including mental illnesses such as eating disorders) that require personal efforts, medical assistance, *and* spiritual intervention.

There are many parallels between what I have gone through during my eating disorder recovery and what I have read about recovery from addiction. This makes sense; an eating disorder is an addiction to control one's own weight. At the most pathological points of my eating disorder, I enjoyed my addiction and

18. James 5:16
19. Luke 5:12
20. Luke 5:13
21. Mark 2:9–12
22. Gospel of Thomas, 9.

Eating Disorders, God, and Addiction

didn't want to let it go. I felt powerful and important, and seeing the number on the scale get smaller gave me a high. Other times, I felt debilitated by my eating disorder, because I viewed doing what my body made me do to survive (eat more) as failure. I never realized it was an addiction until I was recovering, because I actually missed the eating disorder when it was gone. Focusing on my weight had been my method of solving problems that couldn't be solved, my coping mechanism.

One of the most helpful books I read throughout my recovery was *Breathing Under Water: Spirituality and the Twelve Steps*. In this book, Franciscan priest Richard Rohr compares the journey and plight of being a Christian to that of recovery from addiction. He explains how the lessons learned from twelve step recovery programs such as Alcoholics Anonymous can be applied to most human problems or sins. The twelve steps teach us that we cannot solve our problems without the help of God; we are not capable on our own. They also teach us that we are loved and worthy of love despite our problems.

Rohr writes, "God does not love us if we change, he loves us so that we can change."[23] The act of changing, of growing and evolving, is something every person needs to do at some point in life. None of us are perfect; we all have baggage, even if it's not an addiction or an eating disorder. We cannot begin to love ourselves and heal ourselves until we believe in God's love for us. The process of recovering must start with radical self love and forgiveness. This is endorsed by the twelve steps. However, radical self love and healing cannot happen until we apologize for the hurt we have caused to others. Rohr writes, "We usually need to make amends to forgive even ourselves."[24]

Until I thought about my eating disorder as an addiction, I did not fully realize just how much it hurt others. It caused me to lie to my husband and family, such as when I bought a new scale and hid it from Drew or when I had episodes of purging at holiday dinners but pretended to be happy and well. It caused my family

---

23. Rohr, *Breathing Under Water*, 41–42
24. Rohr, *Breathing Under Water*, 68

Skinny or Not, Here I Come

great worry. For many years, I would text or call my mom and sisters every time I "felt fat," begging for reassurance with questions like, "can you tell I've gained weight?" Never did I consider how it made them feel, whether it made them worry about me or think negatively about their own body images. It was always a selfish cry for help. It caused me to be a bad friend at times, such as when I canceled plans with friends because it was easier for me to diet when alone. It caused my husband to have to beg me to eat my meals, worry every time I left the dinner table to go to the bathroom, and miss out on normal things like eating fast food or delivery pizza for dinner.

"Forgiveness is to let go of our hope for a different or better past,"[25] Rohr writes. So much of my addiction caused me to see an enhanced version of my past, to look back at the times I was skinniest and long for those times, when in reality they were the worst times of my life. It has caused me to be in denial about hurting others and hurting myself. In light of this, asking others for forgiveness is one of the twelve steps that I needed to take. Writing this book has given me opportunities to seek this forgiveness from both myself and others. Reflecting on the past brought up many memories for me, and these memories have often prompted me to reach out and apologize.

The last step in the twelve step program involves delivering the message to others. In the words of Rohr, "You are often most gifted to heal others precisely where you yourself were wounded . . . You learn to salve the wounds of others by knowing and remembering how much it hurts to hurt."[26] This spoke to me the most. I have often said to both Gina and Maiya, "I can't let all of this be for nothing." There was the suffering: the agony of self hatred and starvation that I felt on and off for seventeen years, the energy I expended all of that time on dieting and working out and self criticism, and the fragmented relationship with myself that it led to. There was also the hard work: the hours of therapy (often on my only days off, after night shifts when I should have been

---

25. Rohr, *Breathing Under Water*, 48
26. Rohr, *Breathing Under Water*, 69

sleeping), all of the note taking, experimenting, and practicing it took for me to change my eating habits, my thought patterns, and even parts of my identity. In the end, none of it was "for nothing." I am *better*. I am *happier*. I am *healthier*. Yet somehow, this is not enough. I want my recovery to be about more than just me.

My faith tells me that we are called to use our suffering for love, to suffer in communion with others, as Christ did throughout his life and death. The only way I could use the suffering from my sin, my addiction, was through writing about it. Writing this story and sharing it with the world feels risky in some ways. It is a vulnerable thing to do. It is somewhat embarrassing to have all of it "out there," especially when I know many people will not understand or appreciate it. However, when I think about how many people there are who struggle with eating disorders, how many people have admitted to me how often they are unhappy because of their body image, how many people live their lives in endless cycles of dieting; I can't *not* share. I know that my story of recovery will not help everyone who reads about it, but it might help someone. This is how I am choosing to use my suffering for love.

— 8 —

Lessons Learned

As a pediatric resident, I completed a rotation in the subspecialty of adolescent medicine. One of my assignments was to choose a subtopic within adolescent medicine for further research. I chose eating disorders.

In an effort to cover the most important aspects of eating disorders, I read a systematic review about eating disorder recovery. The review cited information about individual types of eating disorders as well as the all-encompassing category of eating disorders. The statistics were not uplifting. I was disappointed to learn that "recovery" from eating disorders, particularly anorexia nervosa and bulimia nervosa, was based on BMI (body mass index). This means that most of the scientific data about eating disorder recovery is about the people who gain weight; it has nothing to do with their thoughts or their feelings. While I agree that weight is sometimes an important part of eating disorder recovery, I know from experience that it does not tell the full story. Sometimes it does not tell much of the story at all.

I have had a normal BMI for most of my eating disorder, and there have been many times during which onlookers would have noticed nothing out of the ordinary in the way of "eating disorder behaviors." For most of my eating disorder, I *rarely* binged and purged, used laxatives, or exercised obsessively; I have also had a normal BMI. For this reason, no medical doctor has ever asked me about my eating habits. By the standards of most of the medical community, I've been "recovered" from my eating disorder since I was fourteen years old.

These are not appropriate parameters for measuring recovery from eating disorders. A systematic review with meta analysis entitled "Residual eating disorder symptoms and clinical features in remitted and recovered eating disorder patients"[1] illustrated this. This paper synthesized information from 64 studies and highlighted the fact that the majority of recovered eating disorder patients have "normal BMI" and many core eating disorder symptoms. These symptoms include a drive for thinness, obsessive-compulsive eating patterns, caloric food restriction, food preoccupations, orthorexia nervosa symptoms (eating only "very healthy" foods and avoiding all other foods), excessive exercise, body dissatisfaction, and continued dieting. In addition, recovered patients have poor mental health across the board, including higher rates of depression, anxiety, body image anxiety, obsessive compulsive disorder and reduced quality of life in psychological, physical, cognitive, work, and school domains.

I also learned that the most evidence-based treatment of adolescents with eating disorders is family based treatment (FBT). While FBT is designed to restore adolescents to health from eating disorders with the support of their parents (by gradual transition of responsibility about food intake from parents to the child), it does not focus on the *cause* of the eating disorder. Instead, FBT takes "an agnostic view" of the cause of the eating disorder, blaming neither the parents nor the adolescent for the development of the illness. It externalizes the illness from the patient, recognizing it as a separate entity from the patient. The therapist is a non-authoritarian in FBT, allowing the patient and the family to guide the process. The primary focus is on stopping "symptoms" of the eating disorder.

In opposition to both of these FBT tenants, I have found it helpful to view my eating disorder as a byproduct of many factors, including my upbringing and my personality traits (i.e. perfectionism, obsessive compulsive tendencies, impulsivity). I do think

1. Tomba *et.al*, 2019

FBT's unique approach to depending on the family to guide initial recovery is incredibly valuable. I am disappointed that I did not have that opportunity when I was an adolescent, especially because the abnormal eating I watched in my family reinforced my eating disorder habits. The focus on correcting the eating disorder symptoms (restriction or binge/purge cycles), while crucial during early recovery, is not enough for full recovery. By many definitions, I have been "recovered" from anorexia since I was fourteen years old. I needed something neither my initial therapists nor FBT would have provided: a relationship with myself.

Observational research studies have demonstrated that adolescents with obesity and adolescents with eating disorders have much in common. Both groups have much higher rates of binge eating and dieting (which seem to go together), come from households with fewer family meals (which are protective against both eating disorders and obesity), and have been exposed to more "weight talk" both at home and among friends. What if we considered obesity another kind of eating disorder, rather than a self-induced and self-indulgent state worthy of shame? I have never met an obese person who didn't feel their life was much less fulfilling than it would be if they were a "normal" weight. Many of them also chronically diet and binge eat. However, instead of providing such patients with support and resources as we do for people with eating disorders, we shame them. Even in the medical community, patients are weighed every time they visit a doctor's office, and they are rarely asked beforehand whether or not this is a trigger for them. They are frequently told that they need to lose weight (as if all of popular culture wasn't telling them enough), and when they diet, the deprivation triggers them to binge eat more.

I believe the *wrong* answers for people with traditional eating disorders and people with obesity are the same. The wrong answers are diets, scales, and exposure to more social media accounts depicting bodies that are thin, curated, or achieved through extreme measures. All of these things fuel self hatred and therefore restrictive eating and binge eating. The *right* answers may be different for different people. If you have an eating disorder, the things that

Lessons Learned

I have shared in this book may not work for you, but they may. I hope you will take what helps and leave the rest.

I believe so many people suffer from eating disorders. Perhaps you are one of them. Do you feel like you are one person and your body is another person? Do you feel like you are in a constant battle against your body's needs and wants and your ego's needs and wants? Do you feel like you have to choose between being confident about your appearance and feeling physically well?

I have been comparing my body to other women's bodies for over a decade. For a long time, I didn't even realize I was doing it. I did it to friends, family members, co-workers. I found it difficult to be in the same room with someone way thinner than me. I now truly believe that bodies are different. I have a friend who is tiny. She is short and thin, and she eats more than me. She has never been on a diet in her life. She says she only regrets eating certain foods if they make her body feel bad afterwards (like the time she ate four cookies at work after lunch). For a long time I was jealous of her body. When we believe that our physical appearance is a product of our talents or work ethic, we fall into a trap of believing certain bodies are better. Bodies are just different, though. It is not up to us what our body wants to be.

In the end, you have to choose. You can change what defines your happiness (your values), or you can make yourself happy again by going on yet another diet. You can decide that you want to be healthy and happy and in this world, or you can decide that shrinking your body is more important. The thing is, every time you shrink your body, you also shrink your love for others, your compassion, and your mind power. When the number gets smaller, your humanity may as well. Even though this is hard, even though you are angry that you aren't as naturally skinny as some people are, even though it's not "fair"; you do have to choose. I hope you will choose life. I hope you will choose love and joy and freedom. I hope you will choose your faith and your career and your relationships. You may not have chosen your body, but God chose to put you in it so that you could be in this world.

Skinny or Not, Here I Come

While writing this book, I read the poem that Sissy wrote about me for the first time. She gave it to me when I told her that I was writing a book. I was amazed at how much she was able to intuit about my eating disorder (and eating disorders in general) at such a young age.

> She yells, She screams,
> Criticizing all she sees.
> Her hopes, Her dreams
> Looking into the mirror
> Crying hysterically.
> Nothing is perfect,
> Therefore it is no good.
> Hating her reflection,
> Everything she sees.
> Unsatisfied from within
> Searching for fulfillment
> Crying out with rage.
> As I sit and listen,
> Helpless and amazed.
> So much potential,
> A great life unlived.
> All she can't see
> Is what truly is:
> Beauty and grace.
> She sees disgrace,
> Not kindness and care;
> She's in despair.
> Talented and smart,
> She lives in the dark . . .
> Breaking my heart.

So many phrases stand out to me now. I'd convinced myself that there were "dormant stages" of my eating disorder throughout my life. Yet even then, when I was fourteen years old, I was stuck in a dark place of self hatred that took away from my joy and my opportunities.

So much potential, a great life unlived. Even as a girl who was not yet a woman (I barely had my period and didn't get my first kiss until spring break that year), I wasted so many of my thoughts

Lessons Learned

on judging and hating my body. I wasted so much of my willpower (which is an impressive force to witness) on dieting, again and again and again. I let my shame about my body eat away at friendships when I believed a friends' body was "better" than mine.

Meanwhile, I could accomplish whatever I chose to accomplish. *All she can't see is what truly is.* I won spelling bees, made perfect grades, and excelled on standardized tests. I played piano beautifully (and even taught myself to write some songs), rivaled the best in the state at debate tournaments, and got a good role in every play I auditioned for. I befriended some of the more eccentric people at my school, didn't engage in gossip or petty drama, and always tried to include those who felt socially ignored.

None of it was enough for me. I went on to graduate as valedictorian, get a full tuition scholarship to the college of my dreams, survive a year of debilitating chemo for childhood bone cancer and go right back to college, fall in love with the man of my dreams, go to medical school, and become a pediatrician. It still wasn't enough when I wasn't thin. I was still *unsatisfied from within*, believing that I was just unsatisfied about my outsides. I was *searching for fulfillment,* truly convinced that I would find it once and for all if I could just have a good body.

It took me sixteen years to come to the realization that my sister had as a seventeen-year-old writing in her diary. My problem was not that I was unable to get the body I wanted; it was that *all [I couldn't] see is what truly [was]: beauty and grace.* I couldn't see the inner beauty and grace that were *me,* the powerful mind, the fighting spirit, and the deeply empathetic soul that always made me *Maggie.* The solution had to be figuring out who I was and what I wanted besides weight loss. It had to be learning to sit with myself, sometimes *in the dark* in the midst of painful emotions and regrets, and learning to love myself. For me, the only place this love could come from was from God. I have had so much love from other people- my family, my husband, my friends, my doctors and nurses, my hometown, and even strangers at times. Love from other people, though, does not make you learn how to love yourself. If self love was not programmed into you as it should have been (perhaps because of your temperament), or if it got deleted (as in childhood trauma), then it can only come from the source of love itself. The source of love is God. God *is* love.

I must pause here to admit that I am hesitant to write a testament of my faith for fear that I will discourage any reader who has different spiritual beliefs than mine. I am not here to tell anyone that their spiritual beliefs or religions are wrong. However, whether you approach Christianity differently than I do, are part of a different religion, or do not endorse any particular beliefs at all; I still believe that you can connect with God regularly and have the opportunity to draw strength from this. Still, no matter how much self love a person has, life brings hardships and suffering.

No matter how beautiful a life is, it is always painful. We are in pain when we are born, when we are pushed out of the birth canal or jerked out of a sliced up uterus, when our blood circulation reroutes itself in order to allow our lungs to begin working, when we become cold and exposed and detached from our source of all life. We are in pain as we grow, as we learn to walk by falling over and over again, as we learn to say goodbye to our parents and spend time with teachers or babysitters. We literally have growing pains as our bones grow during growth spurts. We are in pain as adolescents, through heartbreak after heartbreak, as we figure out the hard way who our "real" friends are, as we learn that we cannot excel in life without hard work. Becoming a woman is painful: the cramps of menstruation, the volatility of emotions associated with our cycles, the discomfort that comes with the first time we make love. Leaving our parents to start a new family is painful (sweet, but painful). Childbirth is painful. Breastfeeding is painful. Learning to balance a career with the rest of a life is painful. Growing older is painful, as we say goodbye to countless people and places we love. Our bodies begin to crumble beneath us, and it hurts. It is life, though, and life is worth it.

My life has been painful at times. An unrelenting perfectionist, I have put myself through pain time and time again, and so did the universe at times. It was painful to have a temperament of perfectionism, to have an inner critic since the age of three that

Lessons Learned

dictated my happiness. It was painful to be in a car accident which broke my jaw and put me in a coma. The resulting wiring-shut of my jaw was painful. It was painful to be in a world that didn't understand me so much of my life- the depth of my emotions, my need for spiritual connection and intellectual stimulation. It was painful to be an anorexic girl at age twelve being force fed by the school nurse in front of my friends. It was painful to have the best year of my life end in a diagnosis of cancer. It was painful to have cancer, and so much more painful to undergo cancer treatment. It was painful to lose friendships during my cancer because some friends found it too painful to be there for me. It was painful to heal because it meant going back to a different world, a world in which I was an adult again and my mother was not by my side constantly. It was painful to find out that my body won't ever make a baby, to go through menopause as a college student. It was painful to graduate from college and become long-distance from the love of my life. It was painful to summon the stamina needed to get through medical school, and to realize that I was *not* the smartest, or even close. At times, it has been painful to be a resident physician, with long hours. It is painful to tell my family and friends that I cannot attend some vacations and weddings.

I have always told myself that I've been able to cope with all the pain of life because I am in touch with my emotions and experience them as they come along; this is a lie. I have coped with all of the pain in my life by replacing it with another sort of pain, a type of pain that allowed me to feel powerful. I, Maggie, a self proclaimed emotionally-intelligent cancer survivor, pediatrician, writer, and Christian, coped with my pain by starving the body that sacrificed so much for me to continue to exist on this earth. It took me this long to realize this.

I wish that I could promise you, and also myself, that my eating disorder is over. I wish I could promise that I would never again look in the mirror and experience crippling body dysmorphia, overeat or under-eat, or cry because an old pair of pants doesn't fit. I wish I could promise that I would never again choose to make myself suffer rather than feeling what I am truly feeling. I wish I could promise that I would never again lose the perspective that I am enough regardless of my physical size or appearance and that I deserve to go through a life experiencing everything with a hefty dose of self love.

I cannot promise these things. What I can promise, however, is that I will continue on this journey, a journey that transcends how much I do or do not eat and how much I do or do not weigh, a journey of self discovery and of self love, a journey of fully participating in this life and all that it brings with it. I will continue on this journey of becoming stronger.

Ready or not—skinny or not—here I come. I hope you will join me.

Bibliography

New American Standard Bible. La Habra, CA: Lockman Foundation, 1997.
Rohr, Richard. *Breathing under Water: Spirituality and the Twelve Steps.* London: Society for Promoting Christian Knowledge, 2018.
Tomba, Elena, Lucia Tecuta, Elisabetta Crocetti, Fabio Squarcio, and Giuliano Tomei. "Residual Eating Disorder Symptoms and Clinical Features in Remitted and Recovered Eating Disorder Patients: A Systematic Review with Meta-Analysis." *International Journal of Eating Disorders* 52.7 (2019) 759–76. https://doi.org/10.1002/eat.23095.

www.ingramcontent.com/pod-product-compliance
Lightning Source LLC
Chambersburg PA
CBHW071201090426
42736CB00012B/2415